RETRIEVING THE AMERICAN PAST

1810–1860

2002 ADVANCED PLACEMENT* EDITION

*AP and Advanced Placement are registered trademarks of
the College Entrance Examination Board, which was not involved
in the production of, and does not endorse, this product.

PEARSON CUSTOM PUBLISHING

Director of Database Publishing: Michael Payne
Acquisitions Editor: Ellen M. Kuhl
Editor: Katherine R. Gretz
Marketing: Kathleen Kourian, Nathan L. Wilbur
Operations Manager: Eric M. Kenney

Cover Art: Christie's Images, Long Island City, NY
Granger Collection, New York, NY

Printed in the United States of America

10 9 8 7 6 5 4 3 2 1

0-536-62530-1

PEARSON CUSTOM PUBLISHING
75 Arlington Street, Suite 300, Boston, MA 02116
Pearson Education Group

Contributors

Contents

Preface to the 2002 AP Edition of *Retrieving the American Past*

To help students prepare for your Advanced Placement Exam in U. S. history, *Retrieving the American Past: 1810–1860, 2002 Advanced Placement Edition* offers a variety of topics and sources culled from nineteenth-century America. This special edition was created from *Retrieving the American Past (RTAP)*, a customizable history reader that allows the college-level instructor to select chapters from more than eighty topics for classroom discussion and analysis. In the college edition, each chapter provides a choice of secondary and primary sources that, together, enable the student to understand and perform the complex tasks of historical analysis and interpretation. This winning combination of flexibility and comprehensiveness, which has propelled *RTAP* to the top of the college textbook market, is now available to the student of Advanced Placement U.S. history.

The chapters included in this special edition have been carefully chosen for the 2002 AP exam. In May of 2001, the Educational Testing Service announced that the Document-Based Question (DBQ) for the 2002 exam would concern a historically significant issue from the time period 1810–1860. Accordingly, the editorial board of *RTAP*, in consultation with AP teachers and graders and members of the Ohio State University History Teaching Institute, selected seven chapters for this edition that individually address some of the most important issues of the period and collectively offer a broad and varied look at the concerns driving the historical profession. You will find the more traditional subjects of diplomacy and politics, as well as newer areas of inquiry such as race, gender, and class. Together, these chapters cover possible topics for the DBQ and indicate the different types of primary sources that the DBQ may include.

All of the chapters in this AP edition of *RTAP* contain primary sources such as diaries, letters, essays, newspaper articles, political cartoons, maps, and other written or visual materials that were created in the historical time period. This edition of *RTAP* also includes an essay on how to answer the DBQ, practice document-based questions, and links to web sites relevant to this period in American history. For more information on *RTAP*, Internet resources in U. S. history, and lesson plans for Advanced Placement history courses, visit the OSU History Teaching Institute web site at http://ohioteach.history.ohio-state.edu/RTAP.

Writing from Documents: The Advanced Placement Essay in American History

Anne Cognard and
Elizabeth MacLeod Walls

INTRODUCTION

You are probably familiar with the axiom, "Learn from the past." Learning from the past is one of the essential purposes behind historical inquiry. Contemporary human behavior, social movements, economic patterns, and government structures all have roots in history—all appeared in one form or another in the earliest of human civilizations and have persisted throughout time. One reason to study history, then, is to recognize our indebtedness to those people, systems, and ideas that have gone before; and learning about human relationships and social structures from the past helps us to understand our own relationships and systems today.

There are other reasons to study history besides what it teaches us about our current way of life. First, studying history is a compelling intellectual pursuit that encourages curiosity, research, hypothesis, and discovery. Second, studying history allows the historian to understand the past better, based on new interpretations of evidence. Although human subjectivity inevitably clouds our perception of history, the job of the historian is to revisit these perceptions, to uncover new evidence, and to create new narratives of the past. For example, much of what we now know about the history of African Americans in the United States is the product of new historical inquiry. One could say the same thing about the fall of the Roman Empire, technological advances in the nineteenth century, or the advent of space exploration in the last fifty years.

Historical inquiry must be both balanced and penetrating. Maintaining such a complex style in historical writing often is difficult. Historians accomplish this by presenting facts in an ordered way, developing a thesis regarding those facts, and using both historical evidence and reasoned interpretation of that evidence to support the thesis. This will be your task as you answer the Document-Based Question of the Advanced Placement exam in U.S. history.

What does it mean to make a historical argument? How can you do so effectively in a short essay based upon texts? This chapter will answer these questions in detail. Along with considering style and arrangement, you will learn how to write a well-crafted argument about a historical subject or event. You will learn to gather and understand facts about your subject, to interpret those facts, to express your interpretation through a thesis, and to support your interpretation with historical evidence. As you come to understand how to write historical essays, you will simultaneously discover what is enjoyable and invigorating about studying history and what we learn about ourselves through such study.

Writing Persuasively

When you construct an argument about history, your primary task is to convince your reader that what you are saying has merit, is grounded in fact, and is a plausible explanation for the connections among or ramifications of a series of historical events or ideas. Your reader must be convinced not only of your purpose, but also of your credibility as a historian in order for your writing to succeed. The best way to convince a reader of your credibility is to demonstrate your knowledge of the subject at hand systematically and consistently throughout your essay. Writing about history in a persuasive manner does not mean that you should use emotional appeals, exaggeration, or digression in order to impress or affect your audience. History writing should always strive for objectivity with the understanding that nobody can provide a purely objective account of history.

Thus, the first element of persuasive writing is credibility: writing with a thorough knowledge and understanding of your subject. A second characteristic in persuasive writing is a clear thesis. The thesis, or central issue of your essay, should be conveyed through careful arrangement of your ideas, which is the third element of persuasive writing. Careful arrangement delivers information deliberately and in a way that best supports your thesis. When you think of writing in a persuasive fashion in your Advanced Placement U.S. history exam, then, remember that your task is first to interpret facts correctly as well as creatively, and second, to convey these facts in as simple and straightforward a manner as possible.

Writing a DBQ Essay

You will write your essay in a compressed amount of time—approximately forty-five minutes for the DBQ. However, the grader of your essay will read and evaluate your work in approximately three minutes. It is important, then, to convey a tone that strikes your reader as controlled, knowledgeable, and energetic from the outset of your essay. Below you will read about important steps in constructing your answer to the DBQ. Although each test-taker will approach DBQ essays differently, in order to write a successful essay you should consider the following suggestions.

Reading the Question

The most important step in answering the DBQ is reading the question. A carefully written question, even one that seems simple and straightforward, demands a good deal from the test-taker. A sample question might read, "Franklin Roosevelt was elected in 1932 because Americans had lost confidence in Herbert Hoover and his policies. Evaluate this statement using the documents and your knowledge of the 1920s and the Great Depression."

What do you notice about this question? First, you should notice what the question is asking you to do in your essay. You are to *evaluate* the very first sentence in the question. What does this mean? Read the first sentence of the question again. This statement has two parts. First, it states that Franklin Roosevelt was elected president in 1932. The second half of the statement makes a judgment about why he was elected. In your essay, you are to evaluate this twofold statement using both the texts provided and your knowledge of the period. Your evaluation of the statement will inevitably be subjective. You will have a specific, individualized response to the judgments made in this statement. But you must support your thesis with evidence derived from the texts and your historical knowledge.

However, you have not finished with reading the question until you have read the corresponding texts. After you have read the question properly, read the texts quickly, taking notes about the important points in each document. The text selections will include eight to ten excerpts from historical documents such as speeches, proclamations, laws, letters, treatises, court cases, cartoons, photographs, and other primary documents from a given period in U.S. history. Once you have given these texts a brief overview, read them again, this time for greater comprehension. Did you miss anything the first time around that you caught during the second reading? If so, take note of these omissions. Also, as you read, consider how the texts are related. How do these texts, when read together, speak to the question? Take note of all relationships that you perceive. Your task is to evaluate these texts together, to understand them as connected and interrelated, and then to develop a thesis about the period of U.S. history represented by these texts.

Evaluating and Using Primary Sources

Evaluating the primary sources in the DBQ section of the exam is an important process that merits further discussion. Your first step in evaluating the texts of a DBQ is to determine the most important information contained in each document—the "facts of record." These are facts presented directly in the documents. In the example of the Great Depression, facts of record would include the events, ideas, people, figures, statistics, and dates discussed in the documents, as well as the solutions that the authors either champion or decry. You might find that certain documents discuss the economic crisis in the United States and Europe, cite figures relating to that crisis, propose solutions to the crisis, and/ or denounce other solutions to the crisis. Although not all the texts you deal with will address all the topics listed above, the documents in the DBQ will share common traits. Your task is to identify and clarify these shared traits.

Once you have gathered the documents' shared facts of record on the Great Depression, you should review the texts for "facts of interpretation"—evidence that conveys something more than just the number of people starving or the extent of the United States' economic downturn. Look for words and statements that: communicate the speaker's/writer's attitude toward the subject; charge the audience/reader with a certain task; attempt to persuade the audience/reader toward a certain viewpoint; elicit emotion from the audience/reader; and present part of an event or idea, but ignore another part of an event or idea. Facts of interpretation require inference and usually emerge from a more careful reading of the document. In other words, in your second reading you are moving from surface facts to facts about the author's or speaker's intention and approach.

When you are writing your answer to the DBQ, you will be asked to analyze several non-text sources. These will be visual sources such as cartoons, photos, paintings, posters, maps, and graphs. In the case of a non-text document, you will be looking for different types of evidence to support your thesis, but you should remember that visual evidence is just as important as textual evidence in writing a quality argument. As you encounter these documents, ask yourself what the images have to do with the subject at issue. List all the objects you see in the picture; take note of any captions that accompany the image; draw conclusions about the caption and its relationship to the image; finally, draw conclusions about the image and its relationship to the other documents you have already read. As you incorporate the image into your argument as evidence, discuss as many aspects of the image as you can, but focus on those that support your thesis. You can approach all the documents in the DBQ section using similar methods. For example, you may encounter a cartoon of Franklin Roosevelt with an exaggerated smile, holding bags of money. You could interpret the message of the cartoon to mean that an optimistic Roosevelt promised to extend a helping hand to America's poor. In contrast, you might argue that the cartoon depicts a wealthy politician oblivious to the hardships of common Americans. Either interpretation might be plausible; you must choose one based on analysis informed by your general knowledge of the period.

Maps, charts, and graphs convey different information than pictures, posters, and cartoons, and therefore should be read and understood differently. Because graphs, maps, and charts convey facts of record, they rarely contain any double meaning. Rather, these kinds of non-text sources are meant to convey information simply and quickly. Your job is to ascertain what information is being conveyed and determine what this information has to do with the subject at issue. If, for example, you are analyzing documents relating to Manifest Destiny, and one document is a map of the Western portion of the United States dating from 1835, you should take note of the map's relationship to the other documents relating to Manifest Destiny. Does the map show the route taken by Lewis and Clark? Does the map show the continuing devastation of Indian tribes as white settlers moved west? You must identify the content of the map, its relationship to the other documents, and, as you would with a poster, picture, or cartoon, its overall connection to your argument.

Interpreting the Facts and Crafting a Thesis

The Document-Based Question requires you to do more than simply gather and understand the facts presented in the documents before you. You must also interpret the facts that you have gathered. After you have read the question and corresponding texts, you should brainstorm about how to answer the question. You will have already identified the most important points of each of the documents and the relationships among the texts. For the first few minutes of brainstorming, consider what sort of approach you want to take in answering the question. A straightforward, and relatively pedestrian, argument involves simply repeating the prompt—suggesting that, indeed, Roosevelt won the election because Americans lost confidence in Hoover and his policies. While this approach may seem appealing, the best papers will move beyond the prompt by complicating and/or enhancing the suggestion made in the initial statement of the question.

Your next step should be writing a thesis statement—your interpretation—that makes an informed argument about the documents. Your interpretation will involve evaluating actions, intentions, effects, and results. You may find that you are working from documents that vary wildly—from a speech given by Herbert Hoover as a candidate for president in 1928, to Hoover's speech to Congress in 1930, to a cartoon mocking Hoover's handling of the Depression written in 1931, to the Census Bureau's statement on government finances between 1929-41, to President Roosevelt's speeches against Hoover and on the Depression between 1936-37. Your task would be to create a thesis statement connecting these various documents. You should strive to do precisely what the question asks you to do: *Evaluate* the statement. If you agree that by 1932 Hoover's policies had alienated Americans, then explain *why* you agree with this statement. What evidence makes you believe this is true? Your interpretation is subjective insofar as it represents your perspective on the facts at issue and the facts about style. But in your interpretation you should strive to be objective as well. That is, you cannot make an unsupported interpretation; your interpretation must be based in fact in order to make a meaningful argument.

Organizing and Writing the Essay

You should order your essay in the following way: an introduction with a clearly-written thesis, followed by a series of support paragraphs with topic sentences relating to your thesis, and a brief conclusion that draws together the evidence and reinforces the thesis.

Your introduction and conclusion should not only be brief but also useful to the essay as a whole. The introduction and conclusion are not merely end pieces that frame the real "meat" of the essay; instead, they serve as important guideposts for your reader. The significance of the introduction to any short essay should be clear: It tells the reader what you will demonstrate in your essay. The introduction also is useful to you, the writer. By establishing your thesis and the basic route you will take to confirm this thesis, you have given yourself a map to follow for the remainder of the essay.

Some students believe the conclusion is less important than the introduction. Conclusions, however, are the last part of the essay the reader sees, and therefore should receive your attention and care. This final impression is what your reader will take away from your essay. Thus, whether you dovetail your final support paragraph into a conclusion to save time, or write a complete conclusion to your essay, be sure to *explain, not reiterate*. Why does your position matter? What have you shown in this essay? Two or three sentences will suffice, as illustrated in the sample essay at the end of this chapter.

As mentioned above, most writers see support paragraphs as the "meat" of the essay, and for good reason. Even with a strong introduction or conclusion, an essay written for the Advanced Placement U.S. history exam will not receive the highest marks without concise and compelling support paragraphs. The most important thing to remember about your support paragraphs is that quality, not quantity, matters most. On a nine-point grading scale, with nine as the highest score, readers will sometimes assign inadequate scores, such as twos or threes, for lengthy essays with vapid or repetitive support paragraphs. In contrast, a solid, concise, clear, and innovative essay that is merely two pages in length might well receive a score of six or seven. Focus, always, on conveying information and supporting your thesis.

Support paragraphs should fulfill the promise of your introduction. As you are writing these paragraphs, be sure to ask yourself: Am I supporting my thesis? Support paragraphs should never stray off the topic or delve into an anecdote that distracts from the task at hand. Moreover, these paragraphs should be so clearly related to your thesis and to one another that, should your reader decide to outline your essay for you, he or she would see a clear correlation between and among all the parts.

In a limited amount of time and in a relatively short essay, you will in all likelihood not be able to devote a paragraph to each text, nor should you. Remember, a simple annotated catalog of the documents without outside evidence is not an essay. Instead, you must write support paragraphs that develop and defend your thesis. These paragraphs should synthesize the information from the sources and your outside knowledge of the topic. For example, you may argue that Americans elected Franklin Roosevelt in 1932 because they were dissatisfied with Hoover's responses to the Great Depression and they believed that Roosevelt could improve conditions in the country. In this example, you might have one support paragraph demonstrating the severity of the economic downturn during Hoover's administration, another paragraph describing Roosevelt's confidence and optimism in the 1932 presidential campaign, and a third paragraph showing Americans' belief that Roosevelt's "New Deal" would end the Depression. Each paragraph should begin with a topic sentence summarizing the information in the paragraph. Your support paragraphs should also contain factual evidence supporting the topic sentence. Ideally, you will have evidence from one or more of the documents and from your knowledge of the historical period. Remember that the organization of your paragraphs should always complement the overall argument of your essay.

It is also in the support paragraphs that your style will come to the fore. While it is always important to maintain a professional, knowledgeable ethos when writing about history, it is also important to show your excitement for the topic at hand. The best essays, as well as the ones that will stand out to a reader encountering hundreds of essays over a period of a few days, will be those that succeed in creating a formal tone while allowing the individual writer to emerge as well. Put simply, focus on getting across the thesis of your essay—this is the chief function of your answer—but do not allow the test format to rob you of your natural exuberance. You are making a claim; do so with vigor as well as clarity.

Part of writing with vigor is using textual support efficiently yet elegantly. Remember that you are urged to read the texts carefully, more than once if you have time, and with careful attention to the most important points of each text. As you write your essay, you will draw upon these most important points, selecting only the texts that directly support your claim. The best essays will integrate texts seamlessly, as though they are mere extensions of the writer's own prose. As you prepare to take the exam, practice integrating texts into your essays in a fluid, yet informative, manner. This is a learned skill, but when learned well, it can mean the difference between an adequate and an inadequate essay in the mind of your reader.

The document-based portion of your exam is designed to test your ability to bring together information derived from three sources: your knowledge of U.S. history, comprehension of the texts given to you in the exam, and your mastery of persuasive writing. Crafting an effective answer to the DBQ is challenging; however, three preparatory steps will help you to write efficiently and well for the exam. First, practice reading and writing exams within a forty- or fifty-minute time span. This will give you a sense of what you can accomplish in that time, and will also train you to read and write in a rhythm that complements exam conditions. Second, review notes, textbooks, and lectures in U.S. history. No amount of manipulation of text in the DBQ will compensate for a general lack of knowledge about U.S. history. Your best preparation for this exam is gathering and retaining knowledge about the subject matter. Finally, understand your writing style and the elements of persuasion.

This final step is perhaps the most difficult, because few study in any detail how they write. Conveying confidence and credibility, however, will not only aid you in writing a coherent essay but will also impress your reader. You can only convey confidence through systematic study of the subject and practice writing the exam. Remember that in the final analysis, this is an exam that tests your writing skills, your knowledge, and your ability to persuade and convey information effectively. As you prepare for the A.P. exam, then, remember that you are enhancing not only your understanding of U.S. history through this preparation, but your skills as a student and scholar as well.

Sample Essay on a Document-Based Question

Below you will see a successful essay responding to a Document-Based Question on the women's suffrage movement. This essay is the length of the average essay written in a forty-minute time span. Before reading the sample essay, use this DBQ as a practice test. Remember to follow the steps outlined above:

- Carefully read the question and the documents
- Determine the "facts of record" and "facts of interpretation" in the documents
- Think about how best to approach the question
- Craft a thesis statement
- Organize your essay: introductory paragraph with thesis statement, support paragraphs, and conclusion
- Write supporting paragraphs that use evidence to support and develop your thesis

When you have finished with your practice essay, compare it to the sample below. How does your essay compare with the sample answer? What could you do to make your essay stronger? Keep in mind that your thesis may be different than the one in the sample. This is okay, as long as you have a thesis that you can defend with historical evidence.

The prompt for this response is: Ratified in 1920, the Nine-teenth Amendment was the culmination of suffragists' decades-long struggle to win the right to vote. What accounts for the suffragists' achievement?

Document A

Source: "The Declaration of Sentiments," by Elizabeth Cady Stanton and Lucretia Mott, statement from the Seneca Falls Convention, 1848.

We hold these truths to be self-evident: that all men and women are created equal; that they are endowed by their Creator with certain inalienable rights; that among these are life, liberty, and the pursuit of happiness; that to secure these rights governments are instituted, deriving their just powers from the consent of the governed. Whenever any form of government becomes destructive of these ends, it is the right of those who suffer from it to refuse allegiance to it, and to insist upon the institution of a new government, laying its foundation on such principles, and organizing its powers in such form, as to them shall seem most likely to effect their safety and happiness. ... [W]hen a long train of abuses and usurpations, pursuing invariably the same object evinces a design to reduce them under absolute despotism, it is their duty to throw off such government, and to provide new guards for their future security. Such has been the patient sufferance of the women under this government, and such is now the necessity which constrains them to demand the equal station to which they are entitled.

Document B

Source: "Ain't I a Woman?" speech by Sojourner Truth, 1851.

That man over there says that women need to be helped into carriages, and lifted over ditches, and to have the best place everywhere. Nobody ever helps me into carriages, or over mud-puddles, or gives me any best place! And ain't I a woman? Look at me! Look at my arm! I have ploughed and planted, and gathered into barns, and no man could head me! And ain't I a woman? I could work as much and eat as much as a man—when I could get it —and bear the lash as well! And ain't I a woman? I have borne thirteen children, and seen them most all sold off to slavery, and when I cried out with my mother's grief, none but Jesus heard me! And ain't I a woman?

Document C

Source: "Social Purity," speech by Susan B. Anthony, 1875.

Marriage, to women as to men, must be a luxury, not a necessity; an incident of life, not all of it. And the only possible way to accomplish this great change is to accord women equal power in the making, shaping and controlling of the circumstances of life. That equality of rights and privileges is vested in the ballot, the symbol of power in a republic. Hence, our first and most urgent demand— that women should be protected in the exercise of their inherent, personal, citizen's right to a voice in the government, municipal, state, national...

Whoever controls work and wages, controls morals. Therefore, we must have women employers, superintendents, committees, legislators; wherever girls go to seek the means of subsistence, there must be some woman. Nay, more; we must have women preachers, lawyers, doctors—that wherever women go to seek counsel— spiritual, legal, physical—there, too, they will be sure to find the best and noblest of their own sex to minister to them.

Document D

Source: "Address of Welcome," speech by Elizabeth Cady Stanton at the International Council of Women, 1888.

Experience has fully proved, that sympathy as a civil agent is vague and powerless until caught and chained in logical propositions and coined into law. When every prayer and tear represents a ballot, the mothers of the race will no longer weep in vain over the miseries of their children. The active interest women are taking in all the great questions of the day is in strong contrast with the apathy and indifference in which we found them half a century ago, and the contrast in their condition between now and then is equally marked....

But we do not intend to rest our case until all our rights are secured, and noting the steps of progress in other countries, on which their various representatives are here to report, we behold with satisfaction everywhere a general uprising of women, demanding higher education and an equal place in the industries of the world. Our gathering here today is highly significant, in its promises of future combined action. When, in the history of the world, was there ever before such an assemblage of able, educated women, celebrated in so many varied walks of life, and feeling their right and ability to discuss the vital questions of social life, religion, and government? When we think of the vantage-ground woman holds to-day, in spite of all the artificial obstacles she has surmounted, we are filled with wonder as to what the future mother of the race will be when free to seek her complete development.

Document E

Source: "Discontented Women," article by Amelia Barr, in *North American Review*, 1896.

But with all its variations of influence and activity there has never been a time in the world's history, when female discontent has assumed so much, and demanded so much, as at the present day; and both the satisfied and the dissatisfied woman may well pause to consider, whether the fierce fever of unrest which has possessed so large a number of the sex is not rather a delirium than a conviction; whether indeed they are not just as foolishly impatient to get out of their Eden, as was the woman Eve six thousand years ago....

Finally, women cannot get behind or beyond their nature, and their nature is to substitute sentiment for reason—a sweet and not unlovely characteristic in womanly ways and places; yet reason, on the whole, is considered a desirable necessity in politics…. Women may cease to be women, but they can never learn to be men, and feminine softness and grace can never do the work of the virile virtues of men. Very fortunately this class of discontented women have not yet been able to endanger existing conditions by combinations analogous to trades-unions; nor is it likely they ever will; because it is doubtful if women, under any circumstances, could combine at all. Certain qualities are necessary for combination, and these qualities are represented in women by their opposites.

Document F

Source: "Election Day!" Cartoon by E. W. Gustin, 1909.

Document G

Source: "An Address Delivered under the auspices of the National American Woman Suffrage Association at the meeting of the House of Governors in Richmond, Virginia, December, 1912," by Mary Johnston.

Your Excellencies, if there are two other things in the world inextricably combined, they are men and women. Neither of us can live without the other. To tell the truth, neither of us wishes to live without the other. We talk of man in the abstract, and of woman in the abstract, and all the time there is no such thing as an abstract man or woman. It is a monster that doesn't exist. Men and women are concrete persons, here and now, human beings anchored and welded together. All men are the sons of women and all women are the daughters of men. Every man here was born of a woman and a man, and every woman here was born of a man and a woman, and we inherit equally from each. And that means, as any biologist will tell you, that we are each. Woman can not contemn [sic] man without contemning [sic] herself, and man cannot contemn [sic] woman without contemning [sic] himself. Man and woman, we are co-heirs, we are kings and queens—not kings with a queen-consort walking behind, but fellow sovereigns—Williams and Marys, Ferdinands and Isabellas!

That is our contention. That is what we stand here today to uphold. That is the heart of the woman movement. That is what, all over the world today, woman, awakened and struggling to her feet, is crying to her mate, is crying to the future!

Document H

Source: Ratification of the Nineteenth Amendment, A. H. Roberts, Governor of Tennessee, 1920.

I, A. H. Roberts, by virtue of the authority vested in me as Governor of the State of Tennessee, and also the authority conferred upon me therein, do certify to the President of the United States, to the Secretary of State of the United States at Washington, District of Columbia, to President of the Senate of the United States, and to the Speaker of the House of Representatives of the United States, that the attached paper is a true and perfect copy of Senate Joint Resolution Number 1, ratifying an amendment to the Constitution of the United States, declaring that the rights of the citizens of the United States to vote shall not be denied or abridged by the United States or by any state on account of sex, and that the Congress shall have power to enforce said article by appropriate legislation, as set out in said resolution; and that same was passed and adopted by the first extra session of the Sixty-First General Assembly of the State of Tennessee, constitutionally called to meet and convened at the Capitol, in the city of Nashville on August 9, 1920, thereby ratifying said proposed Nineteenth Amendment to the said Constitution of the United States of America, in manner and form appearing on the Journals of the two houses of the General Assembly of the State of Tennessee, true, full and correct transcript of all entries pertaining to which said Resolution Number 1, are attached hereto and made part hereof.

In witness whereof, I have hereunto signed my name as Governor of the State of Tennessee, and have affixed hereto the Great Seal of the State of Tennessee, at the Capitol, in the city of Nashville, Tennessee, on this the twenty-fourth day of August, 1920, at 10-17 a.m.

A. H. Roberts

Sample Essay

In 1848, a group of men and women gathered in Seneca Falls, New York, to discuss the status of women in American society. Many historians consider the Seneca Falls convention to be the beginning of the women's suffrage movement in the United States. However, women did not win the right to vote until the ratification of the Nineteenth Amendment in 1920. Suffragists succeeded in earning the right to vote through effective organizing and by emphasizing characteristics, such as strong morality, that distinguished women from men.

In the early years of the suffrage movement, women's rhetoric stressed that men and women deserved the same fundamental political rights. In the "Declaration of Sentiments" at the Seneca Falls Convention, Elizabeth Cady Stanton and Lucretia Mott used ideas from Declaration of Independence to argue for women's right to vote. Whereas the Declaration of Independence had referred only to men, Stanton and Mott asserted that all men *and women* were created equal. Like men, women were "endowed by their Creator with certain inalienable rights." In other words, as men's equals, women too deserved such basic rights as the franchise. Three years later, Sojourner Truth passionately echoed the rhetoric of Seneca Falls in her famous "Ain't I a Woman" speech. Truth described the many hardships she had faced in her life, and explained that she had endured them as well as any man. If she could eat like a man, work like a man, and suffer like a man, should she not enjoy the same rights as a man? Truth's words, however, should not obscure the fact that many white suffragists were not concerned with the equality of African Americans.

The impassioned rhetoric of Truth, Anthony, and Stanton failed to win passage of a suffrage amendment to the U.S. Constitution. However, in the late nineteenth and early twentieth century, improved organizational tactics and modified rhetoric brought women closer to winning the franchise. In 1888, Elizabeth Cady Stanton described with amazement the meeting of the International Council of Women: "when, in the history of the world, was there ever before such an assemblage of able, educated women. . . to discuss the vital questions of social life, religion, and politics?" In 1890, two suffrage groups joined to form the National American Woman Suffrage Association (NAWSA), which would become the largest and most effective suffrage organization. By the end of the decade, the activities of NAWSA helped women earn the right to vote in four western states.

In addition to improving organization in the late nineteenth century, women also modified their rhetorical strategies. Rather than argue that men and women were essentially the same, women began to emphasize qualities that *distinguished* them from men. Women's morality, pacifism, and maternal instincts, they argued, would make them good voters. Susan B. Anthony's speech on social purity exemplifies the idea that women provide moral guidance in society. In the speech, Anthony clings to the rhetoric of equality, arguing that "the equality of rights and privileges is vested in the ballot." But she also describes the special qualities of women, explaining the need for "women employers, superintendents, committees, [and] legislators" in order to control morals. In a speech from 1912, Mary Johnston employs a similar tactic. Johnston explains that men and women are complementary—neither "can live without the other." She invokes the image of "fellow sovereigns" to demonstrate the effectiveness of men and women working together, combining their different strengths.

In 1920, Tennessee ratified the Nineteenth Amendment to the Constitution, ensuring that "the rights of the citizens of the United States to vote shall not be denied or abridged. . . on account of sex." Throughout their extended struggle to earn this basic right, suffragists faced opposition to granting women the right to vote. Political cartoons linked women's suffrage with the destruction of traditional gender roles within the family. Other critics argued that "feminine softness and grace [could] never do the work of the virile virtues of men." The public sphere, they argued, would destroy feminine qualities, rather than benefit from them. But, through appeals to logic and emotion, and effective organizational techniques, suffragists were able to overcome these obstacles, moving the nation closer to equality for all its citizens.

Andrew Jackson and Cherokee Removal

Paul C. Bowers

INTRODUCTION

In the 1830s, the federal government of the United States forced most of the Native Americans living east of the Mississippi off their homelands. Ostensibly intended to relocate these Indians on sparsely populated and less desirable lands to the west; this massive "removal" resulted in the deaths of many. Because the justification for removal was often framed in terms of savage Indians and civilized whites, the forced migration of the Cherokee people earned the most attention at the time and since. Of the Native American people who were finally forced to leave their lands and migrate across the Mississippi River—Choctaw, Cherokee, Creeks, and others—the Cherokee made the most sustained and successful effort to accommodate to the white man's ways. They aided Andrew Jackson in his victory over the Creeks at the pivotal Battle of Horseshoe Bend, 27 March 1814. They made rapid advancement in agriculture, education, and adoption of the Christian religion. In 1827, the Cherokee adopted a written constitution patterned after the Constitution of the United States and claimed to be a sovereign, independent nation with complete jurisdiction over their territory. Neither the federal nor state governments recognized that claim. Ultimately, their efforts to retain their land and freedom were to no avail.

Soon after the Cherokee adopted their constitution, the states in which they resided, especially Georgia, stepped up efforts to gain control of their land. When Andrew Jackson became president of the United States in 1829, he initiated the first major federal effort to relocate Native American populations. His policy, consonant with that of Georgia and other southern states and reflecting the opinions and desires of most white Americans, was to clear the lands east of the Mississippi River for settlement and exploitation by whites.

Jackson's policy was a success. By the Treaty of New Echota, 29 December 1835, a small group of Cherokee leaders ceded the nation's land east of the Mississippi River to the United States for the sum of $5 million and a promise of sufficient land for their resettlement in the west. The treaty bitterly divided the Cherokee into pro- and anti-removal parties and led to the murder, or execution, of John Ridge, Elias Boudinot, and Major Ridge, who favored the treaty, by members of their own nation.

In 1830, Congress passed the Indian Removal Act, which enabled President Jackson to exchange land west of the Mississippi River for tribal territory in the southeastern states. Almost sixteen thousand Cherokee were forced to emigrate, and, according to one estimate, about one-fourth of them died in concentration camps or along the "Trail of Tears," the Cherokee name for the terrible trek west.

How shall we understand what happened to the Cherokee, and indeed to all Native Americans, following the advent and expansion of Europeans in their land? Andrew Jackson has been accused of genocide, as have, of late, Christopher Columbus and all Europeans who invaded, settled, and conquered the Americas.

What is genocide? Webster's New World Dictionary defines it as: "first applied to the attempted killing or extermination of a whole people or nation." You see the key words: "killing," "extermination," "whole people or nation." Was that Andrew Jackson's intent? Or, if not his intent, was it in any case the result of his policy, abetted by the majority of white Americans? If not, why did what happened happen? Jackson himself believed that what happened was tragic but inevitable. So did many of his contemporaries, and so do many today. Jackson believed the removal and deaths of so many Cherokee was the result of the often-repeated clash between civilization and savagery; between a dynamic, superior culture and a backward, inferior one.

Was there no other, better, way? You decide.

THE CONTEMPORARY DEBATE

Although a number of historians have used the word "inevitable" to describe the final victory of Jackson's removal policy, it is important to realize that Indian removal was vigorously debated at the time. For over a decade, the white citizens of the United States, the spokespeople for the federal and state governments, and Native Americans bitterly contested every aspect of state and national action regarding removal and every encroachment of whites into territory claimed by Native Americans. The issues involved in this extended debate—among them the status of Native American nations in the polity of the United States; the constitutional division of power between states and the federal government; the binding nature of treaties between the colonies, states, federal government and Native American peoples; and the moral and ethical nature of removal—remain a focus for often emotional, even violent, disagreement. We who live in the United States of America have not escaped or outlived the consequences of what happened to the Cherokee and their kin. The following selections provide an introduction to the range of opinions, the depth of emotion, and the breadth of significance for this country occasioned by Indian removal in the nineteenth century.

A Benevolent Policy

In his second annual message to Congress, on 6 December 1830, Andrew Jackson explained and defended his policy of Indian removal. Excerpted from A Compilation of the Messages and Papers of the Presidents, 1789–1897, *ed. James D. Richardson (Washington, 1896), 2:519–23.*

It gives me pleasure to announce to Congress that the benevolent policy of the Government, steadily pursued for nearly thirty years, in relation to the removal of the Indians beyond the white settlements is approaching to a happy consummation. Two important tribes have accepted the provision made for their removal at the last session of Congress, and it is believed that their example will induce the remaining tribes also to seek the same obvious advantages.

The consequences of a speedy removal will be important to the United States, to individual States, and to the Indians themselves. The pecuniary advantages which it promises to the Government are the least of its recommendations. It puts an end to all possible danger of collision between the authorities of the General and State Governments on account of the Indians. It will place a dense and civilized population in large tracts of country now occupied by a few savage hunters. By opening the whole territory between Tennessee on the north and Louisiana on the south to the settlement of the whites it will incalculably strengthen the southwestern frontier and render the adjacent States strong enough to repel future invasions without remote aid. It will relieve the whole State of Mississippi and the western part of Alabama of Indian occupancy, and enable those States to advance rapidly in population, wealth, and power. It will separate the Indians from immediate contact with settlements of whites; free them from the power of the States; enable them to pursue happiness in their own way and under their own rude institutions; will retard the progress of decay, which is lessening their numbers, and perhaps cause them gradually, under the protection of the Government and through the influence of good counsels, to cast off their savage habits and become an interesting, civilized, and Christian community. These consequences, some of them so certain and the rest so probable, make the complete execution of the plan sanctioned by Congress at their last session an object of much solicitude.

Toward the aborigines of the country no one can indulge a more friendly feeling than myself, or would go further in attempting to reclaim them from their wandering habits and make them a happy, prosperous people. I have endeavored to impress upon them my own solemn convictions of the duties and powers of the General Government in relation to the State authorities. For the justice of the laws passed by the States within the scope of their reserved powers they are not responsible to this Government. As individuals we may entertain and express our opinions of their acts, but as a Government we have as little right to control them as we have to prescribe laws for other nations.

With a full understanding of the subject, the Choctaw and the Chickasaw tribes have with great unanimity determined to avail themselves of the liberal offers presented by the act of Congress, and have agreed to remove beyond the Mississippi River. Treaties have been made with them, which in due season will be submitted for consideration. In negotiating these treaties they were made to understand their true condition, and they have preferred maintaining their independence in the Western forests to submitting to the laws of the States in which they now reside. These treaties, being probably the last which will ever be made with them, are characterized by great liberality on the part of the Government. They give the Indians a liberal sum in consideration of their removal, and comfortable subsistence on their arrival at their new homes. If it be their real interest to maintain a separate existence, they will there be at liberty to do so without the inconveniences and vexations to which they would unavoidably have been subject in Alabama and Mississippi.

Humanity has often wept over the fate of the aborigines of this country, and Philanthropy has been long busily employed in devising means to avert it, but its progress has never for a moment been arrested, and one by one have many powerful tribes disappeared from the earth. To follow to the tomb the last of his race and to tread on the graves of extinct nations excite melancholy reflections. But true philanthropy reconciles the mind to these vicissitudes as it does to the extinction of one generation to make room for another. In the monuments and fortresses of an unknown people, spread over the extensive regions of the West, we behold the memorials of a once powerful race, which was exterminated or has disappeared to make room for the existing savage tribes. Nor is there anything in this which, upon a comprehensive view of the general interests of the human race, is to be regretted. Philanthropy could not wish to see this continent restored to the condition in which it was found by our forefathers. What good man would prefer a country covered with forests and ranged by a few thousand savages to our extensive Republic, studded with cities, towns, and prosperous farms, embellished with all the improvements which art can devise or industry execute, occupied by more than 12,000,000 happy people, and filled with all the blessings of liberty, civilization, and religion?

The present policy of the Government is but a continuation of the same progressive change by a milder process. The tribes which occupied the countries now constituting the Eastern States were annihilated or have melted away to make room for the whites. The waves of population and civilization are rolling to the westward, and we now propose to acquire the countries occupied by the red men of the South and West by a fair exchange, and, at the expense of the United States, to send them to a land where their existence may be prolonged and perhaps made perpetual. Doubtless it will be painful to leave the graves of their fathers; but what do they more than our ancestors did or than our children are now doing? To better their condition in an unknown land our forefathers left all that was dear in earthly objects. Our children by thousands yearly leave the land of their birth to seek new homes in distant regions. Does Humanity weep at these painful separations from everything, animate and inanimate, with which the young heart has become entwined? Far from it. It is rather a source of joy that our country affords scope where our young population may range unconstrained in body or in mind, developing the power and faculties of man in their highest perfection. These remove hundreds and almost thousands of miles at their own expense, purchase the lands they occupy, and support themselves at their new homes from the moment of their arrival. Can it be cruel in this Government when, by events which it can not control, the Indian is made discontented in his ancient home to purchase his lands, to give him a new and extensive territory, to pay the expense of his removal, and support him a year in his new abode? How many thousands of our own people would gladly embrace the opportunity of removing to the West on such conditions! If the offers made to the Indians were extended to them, they would be hailed with gratitude and joy.

And is it supposed that the wandering savage has a stronger attachment to his home than the settled, civilized Christian? Is it more afflicting to him to leave the graves of his fathers than it is to our brothers and children? Rightly considered, the policy of the General Government toward the red man is not only liberal, but generous. He is unwilling to submit to the laws of the States and mingle with their population. To save him from this alternative, or perhaps utter annihilation, the General Government kindly offers him a new home, and proposes to pay the whole expense of his removal and settlement. . . .

It is, therefore, a duty which this Government owes to the new States to extinguish as soon as possible the Indian title to all lands which Congress themselves have included within their limits. When this is done the duties of the General Government in relation to the States and the Indians within their limits are at an end. The Indians may leave the State or not, as they choose. The purchase of their lands does not alter in the least their personal relations with the State government. No act of the General Government has ever been deemed necessary to give the States jurisdiction over the persons of the Indians. That they possess by virtue of their sovereign power within their own limits in as full a manner before as after the purchase of the Indian lands; nor can this Government add to or diminish it.

May we not hope, therefore, that all good citizens, and none more zealously than those who think the Indians oppressed by subjection to the laws of the States, will unite in attempting to open the eyes of those children of the forest to their true condition, and by a speedy removal to relieve them from all the evils, real or imaginary, present or prospective, with which they may be supposed to be threatened.

A Divisive Policy

The Congress of the United States provided a national forum for debate over the Indian Removal Bill of 1830. Here follows an excerpt from written records of debate in the House of Representatives, presenting the views of Wilson Lumpkin, a Democratic Representative from Georgia and an advocate of removal. The following material is taken from The American Indian and the United States: A Documentary History, *ed. Wilcomb E. Washburn (New York, 1973), 2:1071, 1080–81.*

I differ with my friend from Tennessee [Mr. Bell] in regard to Indian civilization. I entertain no doubt that a remnant of these people may be entirely reclaimed from their native savage habits, and be brought to enter into the full enjoyment of all the blessings of civilized society. It appears to me, we have too many instances of individual improvement amongst the various native tribes of America, to hesitate any longer in determining whether the Indians are susceptible of civilization. Use the proper means, and success will crown your efforts. The means hitherto resorted to by the Government, as well as by individuals, to improve the condition of the Indians, must, from the present state of things, very soon be withheld from these unfortunate people, if they remain in their present abodes; for they will every day be brought into closer contact and conflict with the white population, and this circumstance will diminish the spirit of benevolence and philanthropy towards them which now exists. . . .

But, sir, upon this subject, this Government has been wanting in good faith to Georgia. It has, by its own acts and policy, forced the Indians to remain in Georgia, by the purchase of their lands in the adjoining States, and by holding out to the Indians strong inducements to remain where they are; by the expenditure of vast sums of money, spent in changing the habit of the savage for those of civilized life. All this was in itself right and proper; it has my hearty approbation; but it should not have been done at the expense of Georgia. The Government, long after it was bound to extinguish the title of the Indians to all the lands in Georgia, has actually forced the Cherokees from their lands in other States, settled them upon Georgia lands, and aided in furnishing the means to create the Cherokee aristocracy.

Sir, I blame not the Indians; I commiserate their case. I have considerable acquaintance with the Cherokees, and amongst them I have seen much to admire. To me, they are in many respects an interesting people. If the wicked influence of designing men, veiled in the garb of philanthropy and christian benevolence, should excite the Cherokees to a course that will end in their speedy destruction, I now call upon this Congress, and the whole American people, not to charge the Georgians with this sin; but let it be remembered that it is the fruit of cant and fanaticism, emanating from the land of steady habits, from the boasted progeny of the pilgrims and puritans.

Sir, my State stands charged before this House, before the nation, and before the whole world, with cruelty and oppression towards the Indians. I deny the charge, and demand proof from those who make it.

Excerpt from a speech made in Congress regarding the Indian Removal Bill of 1830, by Wilson Lumpkin, as it appeared in *The American Indian and the United States: A Documentary History*, Volume II, Wilcomb E. Washburn, editor, 1973. Copyright © 1973 by Random House, Inc.

A Breakdown of National Law?

Worcester v. Georgia (1832)
In the Worcester v. Georgia (1832) landmark decision the Supreme Court of the United States and Chief Justice John Marshall found that the state of Georgia had acted unconstitutionally in its assertion of control over Cherokee land. Georgia ignored the court's decision; Andrew Jackson ignored it as well. Taken from Reports of Decisions in the Supreme Court of the United States, *ed. B. R. Curtis (Boston, 1855), 10: 214, 240, 242–44.*

A return to a writ of error from this court to a state court, certified by the clerk of the court which pronounced the judgment, and to which the writ is addressed, and authenticated by the seal of the court, is in conformity to law, and brings the record regularly before this court.

The law of Georgia, which subjected to punishment all white persons residing within the limits of the Cherokee nation, and authorized their arrest within those limits, and their forcible removal therefrom, and their trial in a court of the State, was repugnant to the constitution, treaties, and laws of the United States, and so void; and a judgment against the plaintiff in error, under color of that law, was reversed by this court, under the 25th section of the Judiciary Act, (1 Stats. at Large, 85.)

The relations between the Indian tribes and the United States examined. . . .

From the commencement of our government, congress has passed acts to regulate trade and intercourse with the Indians; which treat them as nations, respect their rights, and manifest a firm purpose to afford that protection which treaties stipulate. All these acts, and especially that of 1802, which is still in force, manifestly consider the several Indian nations as distinct political communities, having territorial boundaries, within which their authority is exclusive, and having a right to all the lands within those boundaries, which is not only acknowledged, but guaranteed by the United States.

"Worcester v. The State of Georgia," (1832) excerpted from *Reports of Decisions in the Supreme Court of the United States,* Vol. 10, published by Little Brown & Company, 1855.

In 1819, congress passed an act for promoting those humane designs of civilizing the neighboring Indians, which had long been cherished by the executive. It enacts, "that, for the purpose of providing against the further decline and final extinction of the Indian tribes adjoining to the frontier settlements of the United States, and for introducing among them the habits and arts of civilization, the President of the United States shall be, and he is hereby authorized, in every case where he shall judge improvement in the habits and condition of such Indians practicable, and that the means of instruction can be introduced with their own consent, to employ capable persons, of good moral character, to instruct them in the mode of agriculture suited to their situation; and for teaching their children in reading, writing, and arithmetic; and for performing such other duties as may be enjoined, according to such instructions and rules as the President may give and prescribe for the regulation of their conduct in the discharge of their duties."

This act avowedly contemplates the preservation of the Indian nations as an object sought by the United States, and proposes to effect this object by civilizing and converting them from hunters into agriculturists. Though the Cherokees had already made considerable progress in this improvement, it cannot be doubted that the general words of the act comprehend them. Their advance in the "habits and arts of civilization," rather encouraged perseverance in the laudable exertions still further to meliorate their condition. This act furnishes strong additional evidence of a settled purpose to fix the Indians in their country by giving them security at home. . . .

The Indian nations had always been considered as distinct, independent political communities, retaining their original natural rights, as the undisputed possessors of the soil, from time immemorial, with the single exception of that imposed by irresistible power, which excluded them from intercourse with any other European potentate than the first discoverer of the coast of the particular region claimed; and this was a restriction which those European potentates imposed on themselves, as well as on the Indians. The very term "nation," so generally applied to them, means "a people distinct from others." The constitution, by declaring treaties already made, as well as those to be made, to be the supreme law of the land, has adopted and sanctioned the previous treaties with the Indian nations, and consequently admits their rank among those powers who are capable of making treaties. The words "treaty" and "nation" are words of our own language, selected in our diplomatic and legislative proceedings, by ourselves, having each a definite and well understood meaning. We have applied them to Indians, as we have applied them to the other nations of the earth. They are applied to all in the same sense. . . .

The Cherokee nation, then, is a distinct community, occupying its own territory, with boundaries accurately described, in which the laws of Georgia can have no force, and which the citizens of Georgia have no right to enter, but with the assent of the Cherokees themselves, or in conformity with treaties and with the acts of congress. The whole intercourse between the United States and this nation is, by our constitution and laws, vested in the government of the United States. . . .

. . . If the review which has been taken be correct, and we think it is, the acts of Georgia are repugnant to the constitution, laws, and treaties of the United States.

They interfere forcibly with the relations established between the United States and the Cherokee nation, the regulation of which, according to the settled principles of our constitution, are committed exclusively to the government of the Union.

They are in direct hostility with treaties, repeated in a succession of years, which mark out the boundary that separates the Cherokee country from Georgia, guarantee to them all the land within their boundary, solemnly pledge the faith of the United States to restrain their citizens from trespassing on it, and recognize the preëxisting power of the nation to govern itself.

They are in equal hostility with the acts of congress for regulating this intercourse, and giving effect to the treaties.

Tragic Decision

Elias Boudinot was a "civilized" Cherokee who, in terms of education, religion, and aspirations, had come far along the white man's path; or so he believed. He agonized over removal, but finally supported it as a last, desperate means of maintaining the existence of his people. His stand cost him his life. The following selection is from editorials written by Boudinot as editor of the Cherokee Phoenix, *reprinted in* Cherokee Editor: The Writings of Elias Boudinot, *ed. Theda Perdue (Knoxville, 1983), 108–9, 142–43.*

[17 June 1829]

From the documents which we this day lay before our readers, there is not a doubt of the kind of policy, which the present administration of the General Government intends to pursue relative to the Indians. President Jackson has, as a neighboring editor remarks, "recognized the doctrine contended for by Georgia in its full extent." It is to be regretted that we were not undeceived long ago, while we were hunters and in our savage state. It appears now from the communication of the Secretary of War to the Cherokee Delegation, that the illustrious Washington, Jefferson, Madison and Monroe were only tantalizing us, when they encouraged us in the pursuit of agriculture and Government, and when they afforded us the protection of the United States, by which we have been preserved to this present time as a nation. Why were we not told long ago, that we could not be permitted to establish a government within the limits of any state? Then we could have borne disappointment much easier than now. The pretext for Georgia to extend her jurisdiction over the Cherokees has always existed. The Cherokees have always had a government of their own. Nothing, however, was said when we were governed by savage laws, when the abominable law of retaliation carried death in our midst, when it was a lawful act to shed the blood of a person charged with witchcraft, when a brother could kill a brother with impunity, or an innocent man suffer for an offending relative. At that time it might have been a matter of charity to have extended over us the mantle of Christian laws & regulations. But how happens it now, after being fostered by the U. States, and advised by great and good men to establish a government of regular law;

Cherokee Indians depicted along the "Trail of Tears" after expulsion from their native lands. (Painting by Robert Lindneux. Original in Wollaroc Museum, Bartesville, Oklahoma. Courtesy of Corbis-Bettmann.)

when the aid and protection of the General Government have been pledged to us; when we, as dutiful "children" of the President, have followed his instructions and advice, and have established for ourselves a government of regular law; when everything looks so promising around us, that a storm is raised by the extension of tyrannical and unchristian laws, which threatens to blast all our rising hopes and expectations?

There is, as would naturally be supposed, a great rejoicing in Georgia. It is a time of "important news"—"gratifying intelligence"—"The Cherokee lands are to be obtained speedily." It is even reported that the Cherokees have come to the conclusion to sell, and move off to the west of the Mississippi—not so fast. We are yet at our homes, at our peaceful firesides, (except those contiguous to Sandtown, Carroll, &c.) attending to our farms and useful occupations. . . .

[12 November 1831]

. . . But alas! no sooner was it made manifest that the Cherokees were becoming strongly attached to the ways and usages of civilized life, than was aroused the opposition of those from whom better things ought to have been expected. No sooner was it known that they had learned the proper use of the earth, and that they were now less likely to dispose of their lands for a mess of pottage, than they came in conflict with the cupidity and self-interest of those who ought to have been their benefactors—Then commenced a series of obstacles hard to overcome, and difficulties intended as a stumbling block, and unthought of before. The "Great Father" of the "red man" has lent his influence to encourage those difficulties. The *guardian* has deprived his *wards* of their rights—The sacred obligations of treaties and laws have been disregarded—The promises of Washington and Jefferson have not been fulfilled. The policy of the United States on Indian affairs has taken a different direction, for no other reason than that the Cherokees have so far become civilized as to appreciate a regular form of Government. They are now deprived of rights they once enjoyed—A neighboring power is now permitted to extend its withering hand over them—Their own laws, intended to regulate their society, to encourage virtue and to suppress vice, must now be abolished, and civilized acts, passed for the purpose of expelling them, must be substituted.—Their intelligent citizens who have been instructed through the means employed by former administrations, and through the efforts of benevolent societies, must be abused and insulted, represented as avaricious, feeding upon the poverty of the common Indians—the hostility of all those who want the Indian lands must be directed against them. That the Cherokees may be kept in ignorance, teachers who had settled among them by the approbation of the Government, for the best of all purposes, have been compelled to leave them by reason of laws unbecoming any civilized nation—Ministers of the Gospel, who might have, at this day of trial, administered to them the consolations of Religion, have been arrested, chained, dragged away before their eyes, tried as felons, and finally immured in prison with thieves and robbers.

Vain Protest

A delegation of Cherokee leaders who opposed the Treaty of New Echota protested to Congress, but in vain. The following excerpt from the "Memorial and Protest of the Cherokee Nation" of 22 June 1836 appears in House Documents, 24th Cong., 1st sess., *vol. 7, Doc. no. 286, CIS US Serial no. 292, microprint, 2–5.*

If it be said that the Cherokees have lost their national character and political existence, as a nation or tribe, by State legislation, then the President and Senate can make no treaty with them; but if they have not, then no treaty can be made for them, binding, without and against their will. Such is the fact, in reference to the instrument intered into at New Echota, in December last. If treaties are to be thus made and enforced, deceptive to the Indians and to the world, purporting to be a contract, when, in truth, wanting the assent of one of the pretended parties, what security would there be for any nation or tribe to retain confidence in the United States? If interest or policy require that the Cherokees be removed, without their consent, from their lands, surely the President and Senate have no constitutional power to accomplish that object. They cannot do it under the power to make treaties, which are contracts, not rules prescribed by a superior, and therefore binding only by the assent of the parties. In the present instance, the assent of the Cherokee nation has not been given, but expressly denied. The President and Senate cannot do it under the power to regulate commerce with the Indian tribes, or intercourse with them, because that belongs to Congress, and so declared by the President, in his message to the Senate of February 22, 1831, relative to the execution of the act to regulate trade and intercourse with the Indian tribes, &c. passed 30th of March, 1802. They cannot do it under any subsisting treaty stipulation with the Cherokee nation. Nor does the peculiar situation of the Cherokees, in reference to the States their necessities and distresses, confer any power upon the President and Senate to alienate their legal rights, or to prescribe the manner and time of their removal.

Without a decision of what ought to be done, under existing circumstances, the question recurs, is the instrument under consideration a contract between the United States and the Cherokee nation? It so purports upon its face, and that falsely. Is that statement so sacred and conclusive that the Cherokee people cannot be heard to deny the fact? They have denied it under their own

---

Excerpt from the "Memorial and Protest of the Cherokee Nation: Memorial of the Cherokee Representatives," reprinted from House Reports, *24th Cong., 1st sess.*, June 22, 1836, Vol. 7, No. 286.

signatures, as the documents herein before referred to will show, and protested against the acts of the unauthorized few, who have arrogated to themselves the right to speak for the nation. The Cherokees have said they will not be bound thereby. The documents submitted to the Senate show, that when the vote was taken upon considering the propositions of the commissioner, there were but seventy-nine for so doing. Then it comes to this: could this small number of persons attending the New Echota meeting, acting in their individual capacity, dispose of the rights and interests of the Cherokee nation, or by any instrument they might sign, confer such power upon the President and Senate?

If the United States are to act as the guardian of the Cherokees, and to treat them as incapable of managing their own affairs, and blind to their true interests, yet this would not furnish power or authority to the President and Senate, as the treaty making power to prescribe the rule for managing their affairs. It may afford a pretence for the legislation of Congress, but none for the ratification of an instrument as a treaty made by a small faction against the protest of the Cherokee people.

That the Cherokees are a distinct people, sovereign to some extent, have a separate political existence as a society, or body politic, and a capability of being contracted with in a national capacity, stands admitted by the uniform practice of the United States from 1785, down to the present day. With them have treaties been made through their chiefs, and distinguished men in primary assemblies, as also with their constituted agents or representatives. That they have not the right to manage their own internal affairs, and to regulate, by treaty, their intercourse with other nations, is a doctrine of modern date. In 1793, Mr. Jefferson said, "I consider our right of pre-emption of the Indian lands, not as amounting to any dominion, or jurisdiction, or paramountship whatever, but merely in the nature of a remainder, after the extinguishment of a present right, which gives us no present right whatever, but of preventing other nations from taking possession, and so defeating our expectancy. That the Indians *have the full, undivided, and independent sovereignty as long as they choose to keep it, and that this may be forever.*" This opinion was recognised and practised upon, by the Government of the United States, through several successive administrations, also recognised by the Supreme Court of the United States, and the several States, when the question has arisen. It has not been the opinion only of jurists, but of politicians, as may be seen from various reports of Secretaries of War—beginning with Gen. Knox, also the correspondence between the British and American ministers at Ghent in the year 1814. If the Cherokees have power to judge of their own interests, and to make treaties, which, it is presumed, will be denied by none, then to make a contract valid, the assent of a majority must be had, expressed by themselves or through their representatives, and the President and Senate have no power to say what their will shall be, for from the laws of nations we learn that "though a nation be obliged to promote, as far as lies in its power, the perfection of others, it is not entitled forcibly to obtrude these good offices on them." Such an attempt would be to violate their natural liberty. Those ambitious Europeans who attacked the American nations, and subjected them to their insatiable avidity of dominion, an order, as they pretended, for civilizing them, and causing them to be instructed in the true religion, (as in the present instance to preserve the Cherokees as a distinct people,) these usurpers grounded themselves on a pretence equally unjust and ridiculous." It is the expressed wish of the Government of the United States to remove the Cherokees to a place west of the Mississippi. That wish is said to be founded in humanity to the Indians. To make their situation more comfortable, and to preserve them as a distinct people. Let facts show how this *benevolent* design has been prosecuted, and how faithful to the spirit and letter has the promise of the President of the United States to the Cherokees been fulfilled—that *"those who remain may be assured of our patronage, our aid, and good neighborhood."* The delegation are not deceived by empty professions, and fear their race is to be destroyed by the mercenary policy of the present day, and their lands wrested from them by physical force; as proof, they will refer to the preamble of an act of the General Assembly of Georgia, in reference to the Cherokees, passed the 2d of December, 1835, where it is said, "from a knowledge of the Indian character, and from the present feelings of these Indians, it is confidently believed, that the right of occupancy of the lands in their possession should be withdrawn, *that it would be a strong inducement to them to treat with the General Government, and consent to a removal to the west;* and whereas, the present Legislature openly avow that their primary object in the measures intended to be pursued *are founded on real humanity to these Indians,* and with a view, in a distant region, to perpetuate them with their old identity of character, *under the paternal care of the Government of the United States;* at the same time frankly disavowing *any selfish or sinister motives towards them in their present legislation."* This is the profession. Let us turn to the practice of *humanity,* to the Cherokees, by the State of Georgia. In violation of the treaties between the United States and the Cherokee nation, that State passed a law requiring all white men, residing in that part of the Cherokee country, in her limits, to take an oath of allegiance to the State of Georgia. For a violation of this law, some of the ministers of Christ, missionaries among the Cherokees, were tried, convicted, and sentenced to hard labor in the penitentiary. Their case may be seen by reference to the records of the Supreme Court of the United States.

Valuable gold mines were discovered upon Cherokee lands, within the chartered limits of Georgia, and the Cherokees commenced working them, and the Legislature of that State interfered by passing an act, making it penal for an Indian to dig for gold within Georgia, no doubt *"frankly disavowing any selfish or sinister motives towards them."* Under this law many Cherokees were arrested, tried, imprisoned, and otherwise abused. Some were even shot in attempting to avoid an arrest; yet the Cherokee people used no violence, but humbly petitioned the Government of the United States for a fulfilment of treaty engagements, to protect them, which was not done, and the answer given that the United States could not interfere. Georgia discovered she was not to be obstructed in carrying out her measures, *"founded on real humanity to these Indians,"* she passed an act directing the Indian country to be surveyed into districts. This excited some alarm, but the Cherokees were quieted with the assurance it would do no harm to survey the country. Another act was shortly after passed, to lay off the country into lots. As yet there was no authority to take possession, but it was not long before a law was made, authorizing a lottery for the lands laid off into lots. In this act the Indians were secured in possession of all the lots touched by their improvements, and the balance of the country allowed to be occupied by white men. This was a direct violation of the 5th article of the treaty of the 27th of February, 1819. The Cherokees made no resistance, still petitioned the United States for protection, and received the same answer that the President could not interpose.

Indian Territorial Cessions and the Trail of Tears

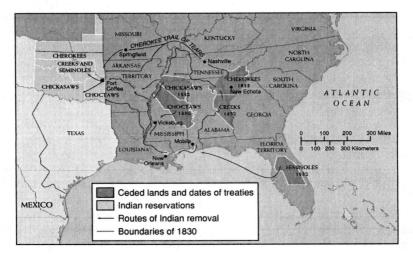

Reprinted with the permission of Prentice Hall from Out of Many: A History of the *American People, Third Edition, by John Mack Faragher, Mari Jo Buhle, Daniel Czitrom, and Susan H. Armitage. Copyright © 2000 by Prentice-Hall, Inc.*

Practice DBQ

Evaluate the forced relocation of the Cherokee and other Indian tribes in the 1830s. What factors led to the removal, and what were the consequences of these actions?

Remember that you should use your knowledge of American history and the primary sources in answering the Document-Based Question. You should take about forty-five minutes to complete your response.

Recommended Web Sites

http://home.flash.net/~kma/treaty.htm
This site includes treaties between the United States and the Chickasaw, Cherokee, Choctaw tribes. Treaties from the 1820s and 1830s show evolution of negotiations between the tribe and the U.S. The treaty between the United States and the Cherokee in 1816 can be compared to a treaty with the Chickasaw at http://www.yale.edu/lawweb/avalon/ntreaty/nt004.htm; the conditions are almost identical.

http://rosecity.net/tears/trail/tearsnht.html
This site has some helpful information about the Trail of Tears. It includes a map of the trail and articles about Indian removal.

http://www.libs.uga.edu/darchive/newspape/cherokee.html
Issues of the *Cherokee Phoenix*, a newspaper in English and Cherokee using the roman alphabet.

http://www.mtholyoke.edu/acad/intrel/andrew.htm
Jackson's message to Congress in defense of Indian Removal.

http://www.mtholyoke.edu/acad/intrel/removal.htm
Read the full text of the Indian Removal Act.

http://www.mtholyoke.edu/acad/intrel/cherokee.htm
Chief Justice John Marshall's decision in *Cherokee Nation v. Georgia*.

The Development of
American Political
Parties, 1815-1840:
The Emergence of
the Whigs and
the Democrats

Jean Harvey Baker

INTRODUCTION

The most significant contribution of Americans to the development of democracy in their own government and in that of other nation-states has been the political party and the associated idea that competition between parties benefits democracy. But the understanding that any rivalry between two or occasionally more organizations encourages citizens' participation and enhances their involvement developed slowly. There is no mention of political parties in the U.S. Constitution. No article considers them; no clause controls their behavior, although today political parties are essential instruments of our government. Nor did the founders from Washington to Adams support such organizations, believing them disruptive factions that infringed on the free choice expected of independent freemen. But even as the leaders of the early Republic claimed that parties threatened the stability of the new nation, their dependence on some kind of organization to run the government, choose leaders, and win elections was apparent. Especially in the U.S. Congress, legislators, including future president James Madison, acted as partisans supporting certain issues and fighting to pass legislation that was opposed by a persistent bloc they understood to be their opponents. But as emerging partisans these early Americans still argued against parties, when they thought of them at all. Their hope was to create a civil society in which factions and discord withered away. In the English poet Alexander Pope's words, "Where order in variety we see/And where, though all things differ, all agree."

For a time—during the so-called Era of Good Feelings from 1817-1825— such harmony ruled. But even during this period the emergence of local divisions over offices and legislation could be glimpsed through the prevailing antiparty rhetoric. The virtues of a permanent organization to contest elections, take positions on issues, bring forth candidates, and even serve as a social association were more and more obvious. Especially during the eight years of Andrew Jackson's presidency (1828-36) a shift in attitude and behavior could be seen, as first the Democrats and then the Whigs created permanent organizations. These early parties were different from the Federalists and Republicans of the previous generation. And while they demonstrated some, though not all, of the crucial characteristics that we have come to associate with modern parties, they were also different from twentieth-century parties. By 1840 the Democrats and the Whigs had developed into national organizations with loyal, disciplined followers, admired leaders, closely fought election contests, and a body of values that separated them—at least in the eye of their supporters—from each other. Whigs and Democrats also came to understand the concept of a loyal opposition in a democratic society, which meant that they might have to alternate power with their opponents. This module will explore how and why Americans changed their minds about parties, and what characterized parties in this Second American Party System.

Contemporary Views of Parties and Voting Patterns

When studying the emergence of parties, it is important to consider not just what historians say but also how contemporaries viewed these new organizations that so quickly became fixed institutions. The primary sources that follow include excerpts from political speeches and party platforms and reveal the attitudes of contemporary politicians. Additionally, a table analyzing voter turnouts is included because it is also crucial to consider the behavior of the all-male and overwhelmingly white electorate. Hence, voting returns should be seen as the testimony of Americans who did not leave written speeches or dissertations about their attitude toward parties. Figures on turnout and party selection display the interest that average American males had in the democratic system fostered by the competition between the Whigs and the Democrats.

Excerpts from Washington's Farewell Address (1796)

To the first generation of Americans, George Washington was indeed a hero. He had been an important commander in the French and Indian War. He had served in the Virginia House of Burgesses and later in the Continental Congress. In 1775 he was unanimously selected to command the Continental Army. Thirteen years later he was, again unanimously, elected president of the United States, a nation that he had done much to help create. After serving two terms and deciding not to seek a third, Washington delivered a farewell address in which he considered some of the main issues facing the nation. Among them was the threat of political parties, which despite his warning, had already developed over differences in Congress. Excerpted from James Richardson, ed., A Compilation of the Messages and Papers of the President *(Washington, 1897), 1:215-19.*

Let me . . . warn you against the baneful effects of party generally . . . the common and continual mischiefs of the spirit of party are sufficient to make it the interest and duty of a wise people to discourage and restrain it. . . . The alternate domination of one faction over another, sharpened by the spirit of revenge natural to party dissension, which in different ages and countries has perpetrated the most horrid enormities, is itself a frightful despotism. . . .

It {the spirit of party} serves always to distract the public councils and enfeeble the public administration. It agitates the community with ill-founded jealousies and false alarms; kindles the animosity of one part against another; foments occasionally riot and insurrection. It opens the door to foreign influence and corruption, which find a facilitated access to the government itself through the channels of party passion. Thus the policy and the will of one country are subjected to the policy and will of another.

There is an opinion that parties in free countries are useful checks upon the administration and serve to keep alive the spirit of liberty . . . in governments of a monarchical cast patriotism may look with indulgence . . . upon the spirit of party. But in those of the popular character, in governments purely elective, it is a spirit not to be encouraged. From their natural tendency it is certain there will always be enough of that spirit for every salutary purpose; and there being constant danger of excess, the effort ought not to be by force of opinion to mitigate and assuage it. A fire not to be quenched, it demands a uniform vigilance to prevent its bursting into a flame, lest, instead of warming, it should consume.

James Monroe and the Period of No Parties

Washington articulated a nearly universal opinion that persisted for a quarter century. Few voices in the early Republic supported the idea of political organizations or the benefits of party competition. At most there were fragmentary suggestions that factions and interest groups were natural expressions of difference. Generally Americans agreed with the Anglo-Irish political writer Edmund Burke that submitting individual preferences to the ideas of a party was a form of servitude. The ideal state followed principles of consensus and harmony, especially in a new political society where it was feared that public contention would shatter the young republic. James Monroe, the fourth president, spoke to this consensus in his first inaugural address delivered in 1817. Excerpted from James Richardson, ed., A Compilation of the Papers and Messages of the Presidents of the United States *(Washington, 1896), 2:10.*

Equally gratifying is it to witness the increased harmony of opinion which pervades our Union. Discord does not belong to our system. Union is recommended as well by the free and benign principles of our Government, extending its blessings to every individual, as by the other eminent advantages attending it. The American people have encountered together great dangers and sustained severe trials with success. They constitute one great family with a common interest. Experience has enlightened us on some questions of essential importance to the country. . . . To promote this harmony in accord with the principles of our republican Government and in a manner to give them the most complete effect, and to advance in all other respects the best interests of our Union, will be the object of my constant and zealous exertions.

A French Visitor Evaluates American Political Parties in 1835

The United States, argued these early leaders, did not need any parties. But increasingly practice did not conform to these ideals. The French aristocrat Alexis de Tocqueville, who had come to assess the American penal system in 1831, recognized the national taste for joining together in associations, some of which were inevitably based on political issues. In Democracy in America, *his famous analysis written in 1835, he discussed what he called "great parties," which were attached to important principles, and "small parties," which in his judgment were little more than interest groups. As a French aristocrat, de Tocqueville was accustomed to political movements during the French Revolution that intended the overthrow of the govern-ment, and from such a perspective almost all the Americans' domestic quarrels seemed "incomprehensible and puerile." Excerpted from Alexis de Tocqueville,* Democracy in America, *ed. J. P. Mayer and Max Lerner (New York, 1966), 122, 162–163.*

. . . The Americans are used to all sorts of elections. Experience has taught them what degree of agitation can be permitted and where whey should stop. The vast extent of the territory over which the inhabitants spread makes collisions between the vari-ous parties less probable and less dangerous there than elsewhere. Up to the present the political circumstances of the nation at election time have presented no real danger.

Nevertheless, one may consider the time of the Presidential election as a moment of national crisis. . . .

Moreover, in the United States as elsewhere, parties feel the need to rally around one man in order more easily to make them-selves understood by the crowd. Generally, therefore, they use the Presidential candidate's name as a symbol; in him they personify their theories. Hence the parties have a great interest in winning the election, not so much in order to make their doctrines triumph by the President-elect's help, as to show, by his election, that their doctrines have gained a majority. . . .

. . . [T]oday there is no sign of great political parties in the United States. There are many parties threatening the future of the Union, but none which seem to attack the actual form of govern-ment and the general course of society. The parties that threaten the union rely not on principles but on material interests. In so vast a land these interests make the provinces into rival nations rather than parties . . .

Lacking great parties, the United States is creeping with small ones and public opinion is broken up ad infinitum about ques-tions of detail. It is impossible to imagine the trouble they take to create parties; it is not an easy matter now. In the United States there is no religious hatred because religion is universally re-spected and no sect is predominant; there is no class hatred be-cause the people is everything . . . ; and there is no public distress to exploit because the physical state of the country offers such an immense scope to industry that man has only to be left to himself to work marvels. . . . Hence all the skill of politicians consists in forming parties; in the United States a politician first tries to see what his own interest is and who have analogous interests which can be grouped around his own; he is next concerned to discover whether by chance there may not be somewhere in the world a doctrine or a principle that could conveniently be placed at the head of the new association to give it the right to put itself forward and circulate freely. . . .

Van Buren Supports Parties of Principles, Not Men

In the following excerpt, one of the chief architects of the Democratic party in the 1820s and 1830s discusses the development of political parties in a letter to newspaper editor Thomas Ritchie of the Richmond Enquirer. *Although the basic philosophy of political party organization was established by this time, its form, such as whether to nominate by convention or caucus, was not yet determined. In this letter Van Buren makes clear his opposition to any one-party system and argues against the "amalgamationist," one-party principles of James Monroe. He is also opposed to any system of politics that sets great men such as General Jackson above parties. Excerpted from* Martin Van Buren to Thomas Ritchie, 13 January 1817, *Martin Van Buren Papers, Library of Congress, Washington, D. C.*

[F]or myself I am not tenacious whether we have a congressional caucus or a general convention, so that we have either; the latter would remove the embarrassment of those who have or profess to have scruples, as to the former [it] would be fresher and perhaps more in unison with the spirit of the times. . . . The following, I think, justly be ranked among its probable advantages: It is the best and probably the only practicable mode of concentrating the entire vote of the opposition and of effecting what is of still great importance, the substantial re-organization of the Old Republican party. 2nd, its first result cannot be doubtful. Mr. Adams occupying the seat and being determined not to surrender it except in extremis will not submit his pretension to the convention . . .

. . . Instead of the question being between a northern and southern man, it would be whether or not the ties, which have heretofore bound together a great political party should be severed.

The difference between the two questions would be found to be immense in the elective field. Although a mere party consideration, it is not on that account to be less likely to be effectual. Considerations of this character not infrequently operate as efficiently as those which bear upon the most important questions of constitutional doctrine. Indeed Gen. Jackson has been so little in public life, that it will be not a little difficult to contrast his opinions on great questions with those of Mr. Adams. His letter to Mr. Monroe operates against him in New York by placing him in one respect on the same footing with the present incumbent. Hence the importance if not necessity of collateral matter to secure him a support there. . . .

We must always have party distinctions and the old ones are the best of which the nature of the case admits. Political combinations between the inhabitants in the different states are unavoidable. . . . The country has since flourished under a party thus constituted and may again. . . . Party attachment in former times furnished a complete antidote for sectional prejudices by producing counteracting feelings. . . .

Lastly, the effect of such a nomination on General Jackson can not fail to be considerable. His election, as the result of his military services without reference to party and so far as he alone is concerned and scarcely to principle would be one thing. His election as the result of a combined and concerted effort of a political party, holding in the main, to certain tenets and opposed to certain prevailing principles might be another and a far different thing. . . .

The press is the great lever by which all great movements in the political world must be sustained.

Van Buren Makes Political Parties an Essential Part of Democracy

Near the end of his life, Martin Van Buren began writing his autobiography. By that time he had served from 1837 to 1841 as president of the United States. Ironically, he had suffered a painful lesson about the power and whims of the political parties that he had done much to create when he was not renominated by the Democrats to be their presidential candidate in 1844. Still, his appreciation of political parties had grown during the period, and he believed that no free country could exist without political parties. Excerpted from John C. Fitzpatrick, ed., "The Autobiography of Martin Van Buren," (New York, 1973), 125.

I have been led to take a more extended notice of this subject by my repugnance to a species of cant against Parties in which too many are apt to indulge when their own side is out of power and to forget when they come in. I have not, I think, been considered even by opponents as particularly rancorous in my party prejudices, and might not perhaps have anything to apprehend from a comparison, in this respect, with my cotemporaries. But knowing, as all men of sense know, that political parties are inseparable from free governments, and that in many and material respects they are highly useful to the country, I never could bring myself for party purposes to deprecate their existence. Doubtless excesses frequently attend them and produce many evils, but not so many as are prevented by the maintenance of their organization and vigilance. The disposition to abuse power, so deeply planted in the human heart, can by no other means be more effectually checked; and it has always therefore struck me as more honorable and manly and more in harmony with the character of our People and of our Institutions to deal with the subject of Political Parties in a sincerer and wiser spirit—to recognize their necessity, to give them the credit they deserve, and to devote ourselves to improve and to elevate the principles and objects of our own and to support it ingenuously and faithfully.

Democratic Party Platforms in 1840

Among the important characteristics of the Whigs and the Democrats of the 1830s and 1840s was their commitment to certain positions that separated them from their opponents. Parties represented principles and purpose and were not just electoral machines based on the idea of electing a certain group of leaders to office. The Anti-Masons, a third party, are often credited with organizing the first national presidential nominating convention. The Democratic party, however, in a meeting held in Baltimore in 1840, adopted what would become an important and recurring practice—that is, a platform that was accepted by delegates to a national party convention. In 1840 Democrats accepted nine resolutions, three of which are included below. From Kirk Porter and Donald Johnson, eds., National Party Platforms, 1840-1964 *(Urbana, Ill., 1966), 2.*

1.   *Resolved*, That the federal government is one of limited powers, derived solely from the constitution, and the grants of power shown therein, ought to be strictly construed by all the depart-

ments and agents of the government, and that it is inexpedient and dangerous to exercise doubtful constitutional powers. . . .

6.   *Resolved,* That congress has no power to charter a national bank; that we believe such an institution one of deadly hostility to the best interests of the country, dangerous to our republican institutions and the liberties of the people, and calculated to place the business of the country within the control of a concentrated money power, and above the laws and the will of the people. . . .

9.   *Resolved,* That the liberal principles embodied by Jefferson in the Declaration of Independence, and sanctioned in the constitution, which makes ours the land of liberty, and the asylum of the oppressed of every nation, have ever been cardinal principles in the democratic faith; and every attempt to abridge the present privilege of becoming citizens, and the owners of soil among us, ought to be resisted with the same spirit which swept the alien and sedition laws from our statute-book.

Mobilizing the Vote

By the 1840s the Whigs and the Democrats were well organized and mounted professional campaigns to get the vote out. Below is one example from 1840 that suggests that the Illinois Whigs were as well organized as any military force. The following is an excerpt from a letter from Abraham Lincoln to Madison Miller. Excerpted from Roy P. Basler, ed., The Collected Works of Abraham Lincoln *(New Brunswick, N.J., 1953), 1:180-81.*

The Whig county committee should

1st. Appoint one person in each county as county captain, and take his pledge to perform promptly all the duties assigned him.

Duties of the County Captain

1st. To procure from the poll-books a separate list for each Precinct of all the names of all those persons who voted the Whig ticket in August.

2nd. To appoint one person in each Precinct as Precinct Captain, and, by a personal interview with him, procure his pledge, to perform promptly all the duties assigned him.

3rd. To deliver to each Precinct Captain the list of names as above, belonging to his Precinct; and also a written list of his duties.

Duties of the Precinct Captain

1st. To divide the list of names delivered him by the County Captain into Sections of ten who reside most convenient to each other.

2nd. To appoint one person of each Section as Section Captain, and by a personal interview with him, procure his pledge to perform promptly all the duties assigned him.

3rd. To deliver to each Section Captain the list of names belonging to his Section and also a written list of his duties.

Duties of the Section Captain

1st. To see each man of his Section face to face, and procure his pledge that he will for no consideration (impossibilities excepted) stay from the polls on the first monday in November; and that he will record his vote as early on the day as possible.

2nd. To add to his Section the name of every person in his vicinity who did not vote with us in August, but who will vote with us in the fall, and take the same pledge of him, as from the others.

3rd. To *task* himself to procure at least the additional names to his Section.

Increasing Turnouts among the Electorate

Below is a table of the turnout among eligible voters in presidential elections that reveals the increasing participation of Americans in elections. Clearly the party system encouraged the enfranchised to take part in a democratic process. From Joel H.Silbey, The American Political Nation, 1838–1893 *(Stanford, 1991), 14, 29, 145.*

NATIONAL VOTING TURNOUT: PRESIDENTIAL ELECTIONS 1800-1840

YEAR	TURNOUT OF ELIGIBLE VOTERS *(Percentage Rounded Off)*
1800	31
1804	25
1808	37
1812	n.a.
1816	21
1820	10
1824	27
1828	57
1832	57
1836	56
1840	80

Changing Suffrage Requirements, by State

Data Source: U.S. Bureau of the Census, Historical Statistics of the United States, Colonial Times to 1957 (1960), p. 681.

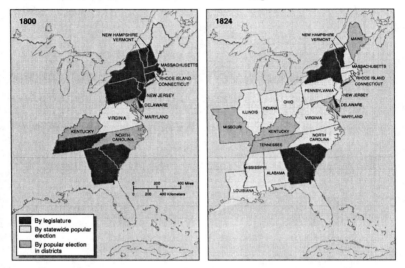

Reprinted with the permission of Prentice Hall from The American Journey: A History of the United States, *Second Edition, by David Goldfield, Carl Abbott, Virginia DeJohn Anderson, Jo Ann E. Argersinger, Peter H. Argersinger, William L. Barney, and Robert M. Weir. Copyright © 2001 by Prentice-Hall, Inc.*

Rise in Voter Turnout, 1824–1860

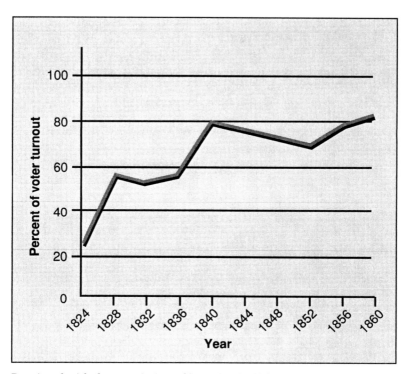

Reprinted with the permission of Prentice Hall from Out of Many: A History of the American People, *Third Edition, by John Mack Faragher, Mari Jo Buhle, Daniel Czitrom, and Susan H. Armitage. Copyright © 2000 by Prentice-Hall, Inc.*

Practice DBQ

Analyze the significant developments in American national politics in the period 1815 to 1840.

Remember that you should use your knowledge of American history and the primary sources in answering the Document-Based Question. You should take about forty-five minutes to complete your response.

Recommended Web Sites

http://ac.acusd.edu/History/classes/civ/jacksonparties.html
Good, brief summary of major differences between the Democratic Party and the Whig Party.

http://www.bartleby.com/124/pres23.html
Andrew Jackson's first inaugural address.

http://odyssey.lib.duke.edu/americavotes/harrison.html
A few images from the 1840 presidential campaign, which show the growing importance of "image" in politics.

The First Women's Rights Movement

Susan M. Hartmann

INTRODUCTION

Examining women's history in the 1830s and 1840s demonstrates the inaccuracy of the term "Jacksonian Democracy" to character-ize that era. At a time when white men achieved full rights of citizenship, women were just beginning their own movement to secure equality. As early as 1642, the New England poet Anne Bradstreet chafed at being denied the full use of her talents, writ-ing, "I am obnoxious to each carping tongue, who sayes, my hand a needle better fits." During the next two centuries, other women expressed their dissatisfaction at being deemed inferior to men, legally subordinated to their fathers and husbands, and barred from intellectual and public pursuits. In the 1840s, these isolated protests swelled into a concerted movement for women's rights.

Feminist activism grew out of women's increasing participa-tion in church-related benevolent societies and in social reform, which claimed substantial numbers of white and free black women in the North. Susan B. Anthony's feminist consciousness origi-nated with her work in the temperance movement, but most women's rights leaders, including Sarah and Angelina Grimké, Elizabeth Cady Stanton, Lucretia Mott, and Lucy Stone, came to women's rights through abolitionism. Although white women dominated the women's rights movement, prominent black aboli-tionists, such as Frederick Douglass and Sojourner Truth, also championed the cause. Women inaugurated their bold and radical movement in 1848 at Seneca Falls, New York, where three hun-dred women and men approved a sweeping list of grievances and demands. Ministers, journalists, and other spokesmen viewed these demands as a radical challenge to the social order and dismissed their advocates as "old maids, whose personal charms were never very attractive," "women who have been badly married," and "hen-pecked husbands." In the face of intense opposition and hostility, the women's rights movement gained converts slowly. Women made piecemeal progress in the North, winning state laws expanding the rights of married women and gaining access to some colleges. But it took seventy-two years to achieve their most controversial demand, the right to vote. Although succeeding waves of feminism have introduced new issues, the women's rights movement of the nineteenth century established goals and arguments that continue to shape the debate over gender roles today.

WOMEN MAKE THE
CASE FOR WOMEN'S RIGHTS

In the 1830s women increasingly wrote and spoke about their condition as women and called on Americans to work against the ideas, laws, and practices that made them second-class citizens. The following documents provide a sampling of the issues that engaged activist women and the arguments they used in their efforts to transform society.

Maria Stewart Claims
the Right of Women to Speak in Public

Maria W. Stewart was born in Connecticut in 1803 and orphaned at the age of five. Although, like most free blacks, she had little opportunity for formal education, she became an eloquent champion of the rights of blacks and women. In fact, she was the first American-born woman to address public audiences. In this selection, an address given in 1833, she challenges the nearly universal opposition to women speaking in public. Taken from "Mrs. Stewart's Farewell Address to Her Friends In the City of Boston," in Black Women in Nineteenth-Century American Life: Their Words, Their Thoughts, Their Feelings, *ed. Bert James Loewenberg and Ruth Bogin (University Park, Pennsylvania, 1976), 198–200.*

I felt that I had a great work to perform; and was in haste to make a profession of my faith in Christ, that I might be about my Father's business. Soon after I made this profession, the Spirit of God came before me, and I spake before many. When going home, reflecting on what I had said, I felt ashamed, and knew not where I should hide myself. A something said within my breast, "press forward, I will be with thee." And my heart made this reply, Lord, if thou wilt be with me, then will I speak for thee so long as I live. And thus far I have every reason to believe that it is the divine influence of the Holy Spirit operating upon my heart. . . .

What if I am a woman; is not the God of ancient times the God of these modern days? Did he not raise up Deborah, to be a mother, and a judge in Israel? Did not queen Esther save the lives of the Jews? And Mary Magdalene first declare the resurrection of Christ from the dead? . . . St. Paul declared that it was a shame for a woman to speak in public, yet our great High Priest and Advocate did not condemn the woman for a more notorious offence than this; neither will he condemn this worthless worm. . . . Did St. Paul but know of our wrongs and deprivations, I presume he would make no objections to our pleading in public for our rights. Again; holy women ministered unto Christ and the apostles; and women of refinement in all ages, more or less, have had a voice in moral, religious and political subjects. . . .

. . . Among the Greeks, women delivered the Oracles; the respect the Romans paid to the Sybils, is well known. The Jews had their prophetesses. The prediction of the Egyptian women obtained much credit at Rome, even under the Emperors. And in the most barbarous nations, all things that have the appearance of being supernatural, the mysteries of religion, the secrets of physic, and the rites of magic, were in the possession of women.

If such women as are here described have once existed, be no longer astonished then, my brethren and friends, that God at this eventful period should raise up your own females to strive, by their example both in public and private, to assist those who are endeavoring to stop the strong current of prejudice that flows so profusely against us at present. No longer ridicule their efforts, it will be counted for sin. For God makes use of feeble means sometimes, to bring about his most exalted purposes. . . .

What if such women as are here described should rise among our sable race? And it is not impossible. For it is not the color of the skin that makes the man or the woman, but the principle formed in the soul. Brilliant wit will shine, come from whence it will; and genius and talent will not hide the brightness of its lustre.

Black Women's Activism

Although Northern black and white women sometimes cooperated in abolitionist activities, they had different priorities. Whereas white women focused singularly on abolition, black women activists pursued a much broader agenda for the elimination of racial injustice. Maria Stewart calls for women to work for the development of the black community in this selection from her pamphlet, "Religion and the Pure Principles of Morality . . . " issued in 1831 and reprinted in Black Women in Nineteenth-Century American Life: Their Words, Their Thoughts, Their Feelings, *ed. Bert James Loewenberg and Ruth Bogin (University Park, Pennsylvania, 1976), 189–90.*

Shall it any longer be said of the daughters of Africa, they have no ambition, they have no force? By no means. Let every female heart become united, and let us raise a fund ourselves; and at the end of one year and a half, we might be able to lay the corner-stone for the building of a High School, that the higher branches of knowledge might be enjoyed by us; and God would raise us up, and enough to aid us in our laudable designs. Let each one strive to excel in good house-wifery, knowing that prudence and economy are the road to wealth. Let us not say, we know this, or, we know that, and practise nothing; but let us practise what we do know.

How long shall the fair daughters of Africa be compelled to bury their minds and talents beneath a load of iron pots and kettles? Until union, knowledge and love begin to flow among us. How long shall a mean set of men flatter us with their smiles, and enrich themselves with our hard earnings; their wives' fingers sparkling with rings, and they themselves laughing at our folly? Until we begin to promote and patronize each other. . . . Do you ask, what can we do? Unite and build a store of your own, if you cannot procure a license. Fill one side with dry goods, and the other with groceries. . . . We have never had an opportunity of displaying our talents; therefore the world thinks we know nothing. . . . Do you ask the

disposition I would have you possess? Possess the spirit of independence. The Americans do, and why should not you? Possess
the spirit of men, bold and enterprising, fearless and undaunted.
Sue for your rights and privileges. Know the reason that you
cannot attain them. Weary them with your importunities. You can
but die, if you make the attempt; and we shall certainly die if you
do not. The Americans have practised nothing but head-work
these 200 years, and we have done their drudgery. And is it not
high time for us to imitate their examples, and practise head-work
too, and keep what we have got, and get what we can? We need
never to think that any body is going to feel interested for us, if we
do not feel interested for ourselves.

Sarah Grimké Challenges the Clergy

*Sarah Grimké and her sister Angelina, daughters of a prominent
Charleston, South Carolina slaveholder, were the first American-born
white women to give public speeches. Their hatred of slavery had driven
them from the South to Philadelphia, where they became Quakers and
leading abolitionists. In this selection, Sarah Grimké responds with
sarcasm and wit to the "Pastoral Letter," a denunciation of women's
public speaking promulgated by a group of clergymen in the Congrega-
tional General Association. Taken from* The Liberator, *6 October 1837.*

DEAR FRIEND,— . . . [T]he Pastoral Letter of the General Association . . . is . . . so extraordinary a document, that when the minds
of men and women become emancipated from the thraldom of
superstition, and 'traditions of men,' it will be recurred to with as
much astonishment as the opinions of Cotton Mather and other
distinguished men of his day, on the subject of witchcraft; nor will
it be deemed less wonderful, that a body of divines should
gravely assemble and endeavor to prove that woman has no right
to 'open her mouth for the dumb,' than it now is that judges
should have sat on the trials of witches, and solemnly condemned
nineteen persons and one dog to death for witchcraft.

But to the letter: it says, 'we invite your attention to the
dangers which at present seem to threaten the FEMALE CHARACTER

with wide-spread and permanent injury.' I rejoice that they have called the attention of my sex to this subject, because I believe if woman investigates it, she will soon discover that danger is impending, though from a totally different source from that which the Association apprehends,—danger from those who, having long held the reins of *usurped* authority, are unwilling to permit us to fill that sphere which God created us to move in, and who have entered into league to crush the immortal mind of woman. I rejoice, because I am persuaded that the rights of woman, like the rights of slaves, need only be examined, to be understood and asserted, even by some of those who are now endeavoring to smother the irrepressible desire for mental and spiritual freedom which glows in the breast of many who hardly dare to speak their sentiments. . . .

No one can desire more earnestly than I do, that woman may move exactly in the sphere which her Creator has assigned her; and I believe her having been displaced from that sphere, has introduced confusion into the world. It is therefore of vast importance to herself, and to all the rational creation, that she should ascertain what are her duties and her privileges as a responsible and immortal being. The New Testament has been referred to, and I am willing to abide by its decisions, and must enter my protest against the false translations of some passages by the MEN who did that work, and against the perverted interpretation by the MEN who undertook to write commentaries thereon. I am inclined to think, when we are admitted to the honor of studying Greek and Hebrew, we shall produce some various readings of the Bible, a little different from those we now have.

I find the Lord Jesus defining the duties of his followers in his sermon on the Mount. . . . giving the same directions to women as to men, never even referring to the distinction now so strenuously insisted upon between masculine and feminine virtues: this is one of the anti-christian 'traditions of men' which are taught instead of the 'commandments of God.' Men and women were CREATED EQUAL: they are both moral and accountable beings, and whatever is right for man to do, is right for woman to do.

But the influence of woman, says the Association, is to be private and unobtrusive; her light is not to shine before man like that of her brethren; but she is passively to let the lords of the creation, as they call themselves, put the bushel over it . . . 'Her influence is the source of mighty power.' This has ever been the language of man since he laid aside the whip as a means to keep woman in subjection. He spares her body, but the war he has waged against her mind, her heart, and her soul, has been no less destructive to her as a moral being. How monstrous is the doctrine that woman is to be dependent on man! Where in all the sacred scriptures is this taught? But, alas, she has too well learned the lesson which he has labored to teach her. She has surrendered her dearest RIGHTS, and been satisfied with the privileges which man has assumed to grant her; whilst he has amused her with the show of power, and absorbed all the reality into himself. He has adorned the creature, whom God gave him as a companion, with baubles and gewgaws, turned her attention to personal attractions, offered incense to her vanity, and made her the instrument of his selfish gratification, a plaything to please his eye, and amuse his hours of leisure. . . . This doctrine of dependence upon man is utterly at variance with the doctrine of the Bible. In that book I find nothing like the softness of woman, nor the sternness of man; both are equally commanded to bring forth the fruits of the Spirit—Love, meekness, gentleness.

. . . [O]ur powers of mind have been crushed, as far as man could do it, our sense of morality has been impaired by his interpretation of our duties, but no where does God say that he made any distinction between us as moral and intelligent beings. . . .

The General Association say that 'when woman assumes the place and tone of man as a public reformer, our care and protection of her seem unnecessary; we put ourselves in self-defence against her, and her character becomes unnatural.' . . . The motto of woman, when she is engaged in the great work of public reformation, should be.—'The Lord is my light and my salvation; whom shall I fear? The Lord is the strength of my life; of whom shall I be afraid?' She must feel, if she feels rightly, that she is fulfilling one of the important duties laid upon her as an accountable being, and that her character, instead of being 'unnatural,' is in exact accordance with the will of Him to whom and to no other, she is responsible for the talents and the gifts confided to her. . . .

And my sex now feel in the dominion so unrighteously exercised over them, under the gentle appellation of protection, that what they have leaned upon has proved a broken reed at best, and oft a spear.

Birth of the Women's Rights Movement: The Seneca Falls Convention

The conflict over women's public participation in the abolitionist move-
ment simmered for a decade and helped to split the antislavery movement
itself. In 1848, two women who still felt the humiliation of their exclu-
sion from the World Antislavery Convention in 1840, Lucretia Mott and
Elizabeth Cady Stanton, called a meeting to discuss women's rights.
Some three hundred people, including about forty men, gathered in
Seneca Falls, New York, on 19 and 20 July 1848. The assembly issued a
broad declaration of grievances and list of demands, drafted primarily by
Stanton and modeled after the Declaration of Independence. The "Decla-
ration of Sentiments" is abridged from History of Woman Suffrage,
ed. Elizabeth Cady Stanton, Susan B. Anthony, and Matilda Joslyn
Gage (Rochester, New York, 1889), 1:70–73.

When, in the course of human events, it becomes necessary
for one portion of the family of man to assume among the people
of the earth a position different from that which they have hitherto
occupied, but one to which the laws of nature and of nature's God
entitle them, a decent respect to the opinions of mankind requires
that they should declare the causes that impel them to such a
course.

We hold these truths to be self-evident: that all men and
women are created equal. . . . [The rest of this paragraph follows
almost exactly the second paragraph of the Declaration of Independence, up to the final sentence.] Such has been the patient
sufferance of the women under this government, and such is now
the necessity which constrains them to demand the equal station
to which they are entitled.

The history of mankind is a history of repeated injuries and
usurpations on the part of man toward woman, having in direct
object the establishment of an absolute tyranny over her. To prove
this, let facts be submitted to a candid world.

He has never permitted her to exercise her inalienable right to
the elective franchise.

He has compelled her to submit to laws, in the formation of
which she had no voice.

He has withheld from her rights which are given to the most ignorant and degraded men—both natives and foreigners.

Having deprived her of this first right of a citizen, the elective franchise, thereby leaving her without representation in the halls of legislation, he has oppressed her on all sides.

He has made her, if married, in the eye of the law, civilly dead.

He has taken from her all right in property, even to the wages she earns.

He has made her, morally, an irresponsible being, as she can commit many crimes with impunity, provided they be done in the presence of her husband. In the covenant of marriage, she is compelled to promise obedience to her husband, he becoming, to all intents and purposes, her master—the law giving him power to deprive her of her liberty, and to administer chastisement.

He has so framed the laws of divorce, as to what shall be the proper causes, and in case of separation, to whom the guardianship of the children shall be given, as to be wholly regardless of the happiness of women—the law, in all cases, going upon a false supposition of the supremacy of man, and giving all power into his hands.

After depriving her of all rights as a married woman, if single, and the owner of property, he has taxed her to support a government which recognizes her only when her property can be made profitable to it.

He has monopolized nearly all the profitable employments, and from those she is permitted to follow, she receives but a scanty remuneration. He closes against her all the avenues to wealth and distinction which he considers most honorable to himself. As a teacher of theology, medicine, or law, she is not known.

He has denied her the facilities for obtaining a thorough education, all colleges being closed against her.

He allows her in Church, as well as State, but a subordinate position, claiming Apostolic authority for her exclusion from the ministry, and, with some exceptions, from any public participation in the affairs of the Church.

He has created a false public sentiment by giving to the world a different code of morals for men and women, by which moral delinquencies which exclude women from society, are not only tolerated, but deemed of little account in man.

He has usurped the prerogative of Jehovah himself, claiming it as his right to assign for her a sphere of action, when that belongs to her conscience and to her God.

He has endeavored, in every way that he could, to destroy her confidence in her own powers, to lessen her self-respect, and to make her willing to lead a dependent and abject life.

Now, in view of this entire disfranchisement of one-half the people of this country, their social and religious degradation—in view of the unjust laws above mentioned, and because women do feel themselves aggrieved, oppressed, and fraudulently deprived of their most sacred rights, we insist that they have immediate admission to all the rights and privileges which belong to them as citizens of the United States.

In entering upon the great work before us, we anticipate no small amount of misconception, misrepresentation, and ridicule; but we shall use every instrumentality within our power to effect our object. We shall employ agents, circulate tracts, petition the State and National legislatures, and endeavor to enlist the pulpit and the press in our behalf. We hope this Convention will be followed by a series of Conventions embracing every part of the country.

The following resolutions were . . . adopted:

WHEREAS, The great precept of nature is conceded to be, that "man shall pursue his own true and substantial happiness." Blackstone in his Commentaries remarks, that this law of Nature being coeval with mankind, and dictated by God himself, is of course superior in obligation to any other. It is binding over all the globe, in all countries and at all times; no human laws are of any validity if contrary to this, and such of them as are valid, derive all their force, and all their validity, and all their authority, mediately and immediately, from this original; therefore,

Resolved, That such laws as conflict, in any way, with the true and substantial happiness of woman, are contrary to the great precept of nature and of no validity. . . .

Resolved, That all laws which prevent woman from occupying such a station in society as her conscience shall dictate, or which place her in a position inferior to that of man, are contrary to the great precept of nature, and therefore of no force or authority.

Resolved, That woman is man's equal—was intended to be so by the Creator, and the highest good of the race demands that she should be recognized as such.

Resolved, That the women of this country ought to be enlightened in regard to the laws under which they live, that they may no longer publish their degradation by declaring themselves satisfied with their present position, nor their ignorance, by asserting that they have all the rights they want.

Resolved, That inasmuch as man, while claiming for himself intellectual superiority, does accord to woman moral superiority, it is pre-eminently his duty to encourage her to speak and teach, as she has an opportunity, in all religious assemblies.

Resolved, That the same amount of virtue, delicacy, and refinement of behavior that is required of woman in the social state, should also be required of man, and the same transgressions should be visited with equal severity on both man and woman.

Resolved, That the objection of indelicacy and impropriety, which is so often brought against woman when she addresses a public audience, comes with a very ill-grace from those who encourage, by their attendance, her appearance on the stage, in the concert, or in feats of the circus.

Resolved, That woman has too long rested satisfied in the circumscribed limits which corrupt customs and a perverted application of the Scriptures have marked out for her, and that it is time she should move in the enlarged sphere which her great Creator has assigned her.

Resolved, That it is the duty of the women of this country to secure to themselves their sacred right to the elective franchise.

Resolved, That the equality of human rights results necessarily from the fact of the identity of the race in capabilities and responsibilities.

Resolved, therefore, That, being invested by the Creator with the same capabilities, and the same consciousness of responsibility for their exercise, it is demonstrably the right and duty of woman, equally with man, to promote every righteous cause by every righteous means; and especially in regard to the great subjects of morals and religion, it is self-evidently her right to participate with her brother in teaching them, both in private and in public, by writing and by speaking, by any instrumentalities proper to be used, and in any assemblies proper to be held; and this being a self-evident truth growing out of the divinely implanted principles of human nature, any custom or authority adverse to it, whether modern or wearing the hoary sanction of antiquity, is to be regarded as a self-evident falsehood, and at war with mankind. . . .

Resolved, That the speedy success of our cause depends upon the zealous and untiring efforts of both men and women, for the overthrow of the monopoly of the pulpit, and for the securing to woman an equal participation with men in the various trades, professions, and commerce.

The Stanton-Anthony Partnership

Elizabeth Cady Stanton and Susan B. Anthony became the most prominent women's rights leaders in the nineteenth century. Married and the mother of seven children, Stanton grew discontented with women's status through her abolitionist work, where she was deeply influenced by the Quaker, Lucretia Mott. Anthony, who never married, was first active in the temperance movement. After the two met in 1851, they forged a personal friendship and public partnership that gave direction to women's rights ideology and agitation throughout the nineteenth century. The following correspondence reflects the nature of their relationship and the burden that women's traditional domestic responsibilities placed on their public work. Taken from Elizabeth Cady Stanton As Revealed in Her Letters, Diary and Reminiscences, *ed. Theodore Stanton and Harriot Stanton Blatch (New York, 1922), 2:41–42, 54–55, 59–60, 64–67, 70–71.*

Stanton to Anthony, April 2, 1852

Men and angels give me patience! I am at the boiling point! If I do not find some day the use of my tongue on this question, I shall die of an intellectual repression, a woman's rights convulsion! Oh, Susan! Susan! Susan! You must manage to spend a week with me before the Rochester convention, for I am afraid that I cannot attend it; I have so much care with all these boys on my hands. But I will write a letter. How much I do long to be free from

---

housekeeping and children, so as to have some time to read, and think, and write. But it may be well for me to understand all the trials of woman's lot, that I may more eloquently proclaim them when the time comes.

Stanton to Anthony, Dec. 1, 1853

Can you get any acute lawyer . . . sufficiently interested in our movement to look up just eight laws concerning us—the very worst in all the code? I can generalize and philosophize easily enough of myself; but the details of the particular laws I need, I have not time to look up. You see, while I am about the house, surrounded by my children, washing dishes, baking, sewing, etc., I can think up many points, but I cannot search books, for my hands as well as my brains would be necessary for that work. . . . I seldom have one hour undisturbed in which to sit down and write. Men who can, when they wish to write a document, shut themselves up for days with their thoughts and their books, know little of what difficulties a woman must surmount to get off a tolerable production.

Stanton to Anthony, September 10, 1855

I wish that I were as free as you and I would stump the state

The great suffrage team, Susan B. Anthony and Elizabeth Cady Stanton, pose together in 1870, the year they founded the National Woman Suffrage Association (Courtesy of The Schlesinger Library.)

in a twinkling. But I am not, and what is more, I passed through a terrible scourging when last at my father's. I cannot tell you how deep the iron entered my soul. I never felt more keenly the degradation of my sex. To think that all in me of which my father would have felt a proper pride had I been a man, is deeply mortifying to him because I am a woman. That thought has stung me to a fierce decision—to speak as soon as I can do myself credit. But the pressure on me just now is too great. Henry sides with my friends, who oppose me in all that is dearest to my heart. They are not willing that I should write even on the woman question. But I will both write and speak.

Anthony to Stanton, June 5, 1856

And, Mrs. Stanton, not a word on that Address for the Teachers' Convention. This week was to be leisure to me, and the Mercy only knows when I can get a moment; and what is worse, as the Lord knows full well, if I get all the time the world has, I can't get up a decent document. Oh, dear, dear! There is so much to say and I am so without constructive power to put in symmetrical order. So, for the love of me and for the saving of the reputation of womanhood, I beg you, with one baby on your knee and another at your feet, and four boys whistling, buzzing, hallooing "Ma, Ma," set yourself about the work. It is of but small moment who writes the Address, but of vast moment that it be well done. Ah! Mrs. Stanton, don't say No, nor don't delay it a moment; for I must have it all done and almost commit to memory. . . . Don't delay one mail to tell me what you will do, for I must not and will not allow these schoolmasters to say: "See, these women can't or won't do anything when we do give them a chance." . . . Now do, I pray you, give heed to my prayer. Those of you who have the talent to do honor to poor—oh! how poor—womanhood, have all given yourself over to baby-making; and left poor brainless me to do battle alone. It is a shame. Such a body as I might be spared to rock cradles. But it is a crime for you and Lucy Stone and Antoinette Brown to be doing it. I have just engaged to attend a progressive meeting in Erie County, the first of September, just because there is no other woman to be had, but not because I feel in the least competent.

Stanton to Anthony, June 10, 1856

Your servant is not dead but liveth. Imagine me, day in and day out, watching, bathing, dressing, nursing, and promenading the precious contents of a little crib in the corner of the room. I pace up and down these two chambers of mine like a caged lioness, longing to bring to a close nursing and housekeeping cares.... Is your speech to be exclusively on the point of educating the sexes together, or as to the best manner of educating women? I will do what I can to help you with your lecture. Let Lucy and Antoinette rest awhile in peace and quietness and think great thoughts for the future. It is not well to be in the excitement of public life all the time; do not keep stirring them up or mourning over their repose. You need rest too, Susan. Let the world alone awhile. We cannot bring about a moral revolution in a day or year. Now that I have two daughters, I feel fresh strength to work. It is not in vain that in myself I have experienced all the wearisome cares to which woman in her best estate is subject.

Stanton to Anthony, July 20, 1857

A man in marrying gives up no right; but a woman, every right, even the most sacred of all—the right to her own person. There will be no response among women to our demands until we have first aroused in them a sense of personal dignity and independence; and so long as our present false marriage relation continues, which in most cases is nothing more nor less than legalized prostitution, woman can have no self-respect, and of course man will have none for her; for the world estimates us according to the value we put upon ourselves. Personal freedom is the first right to be proclaimed, and that does not and cannot now belong to the relation of wife, to the mistress of the isolated home, to the financial dependent.

Stanton to Anthony, August 20, 1857

DEAR SUSAN,—I did indeed see by the papers that you had once more stirred that part of intellectual stagnation, the educational convention. The *Times* was really quite complimentary. Henry brought me every item he could see about you. "Well," he would say, "another notice about Susan. You stir up Susan, and she stirs the world." What a set of fools those schoolmarms must be! Well, if in order to please men they wish to live on air, let them. I was glad you went to torment them. I will do anything to help you on. If I do nothing else this fall I am bound to aid you to get up an antislavery address. You must come here for a week or two and we will accomplish wonders. You and I have a prospect of a good long life. We shall not be in our prime before fifty, and after that we shall be good for twenty years at least.

Practice DBQ

Evaluate the movement for women's rights in the 1830s and 1840s. What tactics and arguments were used in this movement, and were they successful?

Remember that you should use your knowledge of American history and the primary sources in answering the Document-Based Question. You should take about forty-five minutes to complete your response.

Recommended Web Sites

http://www.tncrimlaw.com/civil_bible/seneca_falls.htm
This site contains the complete text of the Seneca Falls "Declaration of Sentiments."

http://www.loc.gov/exhibits/treasures/trr040.html
Contains material from Elizabeth Cady Stanton's 1848 scrapbook, including Stanton's handwritten notes and informative newspaper clippings.

http://lcweb.loc.gov/exhibits/african/afam006.html
This site on abolitionism includes images of anti-slavery newspapers.

http://jefferson.village.virginia.edu/seminar/unit3/grimke.htm
Very brief excerpt from Angelina Grimke's "Appeal to the Christian Women of the South"; the full text is available at http://history.furman.edu/~benson/docs/grimke2.htm.

http://www.fordham.edu/halsall/mod/douglass-hypo.html
Read Frederick Douglass's speech denouncing slavery.

http://www.pbs.org/wgbh/aia/part4/index.html
Good historical documents on antebellum slavery, abolitionism, fugitive slave law, westward expansion, and events leading to the Civil War. See, for example, Angelina Grimke's speech in Pennsylvania at http://www.pbs.org/wgbh/aia/part4/4h2939.html.

Manifest Destiny

Peter L. Hahn and Michael J. Hogan

INTRODUCTION

During the 1840s, the United States acquired control over vast tracts of land in Texas, the southwest, including California, and the Oregon Territory. Some of the land was acquired by diplomacy and some by force; all of it has remained an integral part of the country. Some Americans advocated and celebrated such enormous territorial growth by rallying behind a sense of national mission and exceptionalism called "Manifest Destiny" and supporting war against Mexico as a means to continental empire. Others opposed this expansionism on political, economic, strategic, and moral grounds. Such controversy over expansionism has persisted since the 1840s.

The Contemporary Debate over Continental Expansion

The following documents reveal many aspects of the debate on expansionism that began in the 1830s and persisted into the 1840s. The first two documents offer contrasting views of the general question of expansionism. The remaining documents reveal the parameters of debate as it focused on specific issues: whether to annex Texas in 1844, whether to wage war on Mexico in 1846–1848, and whether to permit slavery to spread into the territories acquired. Collectively, these records demonstrate that the American people reached no consensus either in favor of, or in opposition to, the expansionism that occurred.

John L. O'Sullivan
Advocates Manifest Destiny

An intellectual atmosphere conducive to expansionism stood behind the United States's drive across the continent in the 1840s. Some of the strongest advocates of expansion and conquest were writers of editorials in the popular press, and of these perhaps the most famous was John L. O'Sullivan, editor of The United States Magazine and Democratic Review. *The selection printed below, comprised of parts of two O'Sullivan editorials published in 1839 and 1845, conveys the themes and tone of O'Sullivan's advocacy. The editorials originally appeared in* The United States Magazine and Democratic Review, *6 (November 1839):426–27, 429–30; and 17 (July 1845):5, 7–8.*

[1839]

The American people having derived their origin from many other nations, and the Declaration of National Independence being entirely based on the great principle of human equality, these facts demonstrate at once our disconnected position as regards any other nation; that we have, in reality, but little connection with the past history of any of them, and still less with all antiquity, its glories, or its crimes. On the contrary, our national birth was the beginning of a new history, the formation and progress of an untried political system, which separates us from the past and connects us with the future only; and so far as regards the entire development of the natural rights of man, in moral, political, and national life, we may confidently assume that our country is destined to be *the great nation* of futurity. . . .

We have no interest in the scenes of antiquity, only as lessons of avoidance of nearly all their examples. The expansive future is our arena, and for our history. We are entering on its untrodden space, with the truths of God in our minds, beneficent objects in our hearts, and with a clear conscience unsullied by the past. We are the nation of human progress, and who will, what can, set limits to our onward march? Providence is with us, and no earthly power can. We point to the everlasting truth on the first page of our national declaration, and we proclaim to the millions of other lands, that "the gates of hell"—the powers of aristocracy and monarchy—"shall not prevail against it."

The far-reaching, the boundless future will be the era of American greatness. In its magnificent domain of space and time, the nation of many nations is destined to manifest to mankind the excellence of divine principles; to establish on earth the noblest temple ever dedicated to the worship of the Most High—the Sacred and the True. Its floor shall be a hemisphere—its roof the firmament of the star-studded heavens, and its congregation an Union of many Republics, comprising hundreds of happy millions, calling, owning no man master, but governed by God's natural and moral law of equality, the law of brotherhood—of "peace and good will amongst men.". . .

Yes, we are the nation of progress, of individual freedom, of universal enfranchisement. Equality of rights is the cynosure of our union of States, the grand exemplar of the correlative equality of individuals; and while truth sheds its effulgence, we cannot retrograde, without dissolving the one and subverting the other.

We must onward to the fulfilment of our mission—to the entire development of the principle of our organization—freedom of conscience, freedom of person, freedom of trade and business pursuits, universality of freedom and equality. This is our high destiny, and in nature's eternal, inevitable decree of cause and effect we must accomplish it. All this will be our future history, to establish on earth the moral dignity and salvation of man—the immutable truth and beneficence of God. For this blessed mission to the nations of the world, which are shut out from the life-giving light of truth, has America been chosen; and her high example shall smite unto death the tyranny of kings, hierarchs, and oligarchs, and carry the glad tidings of peace and good will where myriads now endure an existence scarcely more enviable than that of beasts of the field. Who, then, can doubt that our country is destined to be *the great nation* of futurity?

[1845]

It is time now for opposition to the Annexation of Texas to cease, all further agitation of the waters of bitterness and strife, at least in connexion with this question,—even though it may perhaps be required of us as a necessary condition of the freedom of our institutions, that we must live on for ever in a state of unpausing struggle and excitement upon some subject of party division or other. But, in regard to Texas, enough has now been given to Party. It is time for the common duty of Patriotism to the Country to succeed;—or if this claim will not be recognized, it is at least time for common sense to acquiesce with decent grace in the inevitable and the irrevocable.

Texas is now ours. Already, before these words are written, her Convention has undoubtedly ratified the acceptance, by her Congress, of our proffered invitation into the Union; and made the requisite changes in her already republican form of constitution to adopt it to its future federal relations. Her star and her stripe may already be said to have taken their place in the glorious blazon of our common nationality; and the sweep of our eagle's wing already includes within its circuit the wide extent of her fair and fertile land. She is no longer to us a mere geographical space—a certain combination of coast, plain, mountain, valley, forest and stream. She is no longer to us a mere country on the map. She comes within the dear and sacred designation of Our Country; no longer a *"pays,"* [country] she is part of *"la patrie;"*

[the nation] and that which is at once a sentiment and a virtue, Patriotism, already begins to thrill for her too within the national heart. . . .

Why, were other reasoning wanting, in favor of now elevating this question of the reception of Texas into the Union, out of the lower region of our past party dissensions, up to its proper level of a high and broad nationality, it surely is to be found, found abundantly, in the manner in which other nations have undertaken to intrude themselves into it, between us and the proper parties to the case, in a spirit of hostile interference against us, for the avowed object of thwarting our policy and hampering our power, limiting our greatness and checking the fulfilment of our manifest destiny to overspread the continent allotted by Providence for the free development of our yearly multiplying millions. This we have seen done by England, our old rival and enemy; and by France. . . .

. . . Texas has been absorbed into the Union in the inevitable fulfilment of the general law which is rolling our population westward; the connexion of which with that ratio of growth in population which is destined within a hundred years to swell our numbers to the enormous population of *two hundred and fifty millions* (if not more), is too evident to leave us in doubt of the manifest design of Providence in regard to the occupation of this continent. It was disintegrated from Mexico in the natural course of events, by a process perfectly legitimate on its own part, blameless on ours; and in which all the censures due to wrong, perfidy and folly, rest on Mexico alone. And possessed as it was by a population which was in truth but a colonial detachment from our own, and which was still bound by myriad ties of the very heartstrings to its old relations, domestic and political, their incorporation into the Union was not only inevitable, but the most natural, right and proper thing in the world—and it is only astonishing that there should be any among ourselves to say it nay.

W. E. Channing Denounces Expansion

Of course, not all Americans endorsed the annexation of Texas or the general pattern of continental expansion. Many Americans opposed this territorial growth on the grounds that it would undermine democratic institutions at home, estrange relations with foreign states, encourage the spread of slavery, and violate the country's deepest values, such as peace and the rule of law. Boston minister William Ellery Channing emerged as a leading anti-expansionist spokesman during the national debate on the Republic of Texas's request for annexation in 1837, a request that, at first, was denied. The selection below is taken from Channing's letter of August 1837 to Henry Clay. Excerpted from The Works of William E. Channing, D.D., *6th edition, (Boston, 1846), 2:183–87, 204–8, 210, 217–18, 220, 231–32, 240.*

MY DEAR SIR,

. . . It is with great reluctance that I enter on the topic of this letter. . . . I desire nothing so much as to devote what remains of life to the study and exposition of great principles and universal truths. But the subject of Texas weighs heavily on my mind, and I cannot shake it off. To me, it is more than a political question. It belongs eminently to morals and religion. . . . Should Texas be annexed to our country, I feel that I could not forgive myself, if, with my deep, solemn impressions, I should do nothing to avert the evil. I cannot easily believe, that this disastrous measure is to be adopted, especially at the present moment. The annexation of Texas, under existing circumstances, would be more than rashness; it would be madness. That opposition to it must exist at the South, as well as at the North, I cannot doubt. Still, there is a general impression, that great efforts will be made to accomplish this object at the approaching session of Congress, and that nothing but strenuous resistance can prevent their success. I must write, therefore, as if the danger were real and imminent; and if any should think that I am betrayed into undue earnestness by a false alarm, they will remember that there are circumstances, in which excess of vigilance is a virtue. . . .

We have a strong argument against annexing Texas to the United States, in the Criminality of the revolt which threatens to sever that country from Mexico. On this point our citizens need light. The Texan insurrection is seriously regarded by many among us as a struggle of the oppressed for freedom. The Texan revolution is thought to resemble our own. Our own is contaminated by being brought into such relationship, and we owe to our fathers and ourselves a disclaimer of affinity with this new republic. The Texan revolt, if regarded in its causes and its means of success, is criminal; and we ought in no way to become partakers in its guilt. . . .

Having unfolded the argument against the annexation of Texas from the criminality of the revolt, I proceed to a second very solemn consideration, namely, that by this act our country will enter on a career of encroachment, war, and crime, and will merit and incur the punishment and woe of aggravated wrong-doing. The seizure of Texas will not stand alone. It will darken our future history. It will be linked by an iron necessity to long-continued deeds of rapine and blood. Ages may not see the catastrophe of the tragedy, the first scene of which we are so ready to enact. It is strange that nations should be so much more rash than individuals; and this, in the face of experience, which has been teaching, from the beginning of society, that, of all precipitate and criminal deeds, those perpetrated by nations are the most fruitful of misery.

Did this country know itself, or were it disposed to profit by self-knowledge, it would feel the necessity of laying an immediate curb on its passion for extended territory. It would not trust itself to new acquisitions. It would shrink from the temptation to conquest. We are a restless people, prone to encroachment, impatient of the ordinary laws of progress, less anxious to consolidate and perfect than to extend our institutions, more ambitious of spreading ourselves over a wide space than of diffusing beauty and fruitfulness over a narrower field. We boast of our rapid growth, forgetting that, throughout nature, noble growths are slow. Our people throw themselves beyond the bounds of civilization, and expose themselves to relapses into a semi-barbarous state, under the impulse of wild imagination, and for the name of great possessions. . . .

It is full time, that we should lay on ourselves serious, resolute restraint. Possessed of a domain, vast enough for the growth of ages, it is time for us to stop in the career of acquisition and conquest. Already endangered by our greatness, we cannot advance without imminent peril to our institutions, union, prosperity, virtue, and peace. . . .

Even were the dispositions of our government most pacific and opposed to encroachment, the annexation of Texas would almost certainly embroil us with Mexico. This territory would be overrun by adventurers; and the most unprincipled of these, the proscribed, the disgraced, the outcasts of society, would, of course, keep always in advance of the better population. These would represent our republic on the borders of the Mexican States. The history of the connexion of such men with the Indians, forewarns us of the outrages which would attend their contact with the border inhabitants of our southern neighbour. . . .

Hitherto I have spoken of the annexation of Texas as embroiling us with Mexico; but it will not stop here. It will bring us into collision with other states. It will, almost of necessity, involve us in hostility with European powers. . . .

I proceed now to a consideration of what is to me the strongest argument against annexing Texas to the United States. . . . The annexation of Texas, I have said, will extend and perpetuate slavery. It is fitted, and, still more, intended to do so. On this point there can be no doubt. . . .

I now ask, whether, as a people, we are prepared to seize on a neighbouring territory for the end of extending slavery? I ask, whether, as a people, we can stand forth in the sight of God, in the sight of the nations, and adopt this atrocious policy? Sooner perish! Sooner be our name blotted out from the record of nations! . . .

I now proceed to another important argument against the annexation of Texas to our country, the argument drawn from the bearings of the measure on our National Union. Next to liberty, union is our great political interest, and this cannot but be loosened, it may be dissolved, by the proposed extension of our territory. . . .

I proceed now to the last head of this communication. I observe, that the cause of Liberty, of free institutions, a cause more sacred than union, forbids the annexation of Texas. It is plain from the whole preceding discussion, that this measure will exert a disastrous influence on the moral sentiments and principles of this country, by sanctioning plunder, by inflaming cupidity, by encouraging lawless speculation, by bringing into the confederacy a community whose whole history and circumstances are adverse to moral order and wholesome restraint, by violating national faith, by proposing immoral and inhuman ends, by placing us as a people in opposition to the efforts of philanthropy, and the advancing movements of the civilized world. It will spread a moral corruption, already too rife among us, and, in so doing, it will shake the foundations of freedom at home, and bring reproach on it abroad. It will be treachery to the great cause which has been confided to this above all nations.

Polk Asks for War on Mexico

Nine months after the Senate rejected the annexation treaty, lame-duck President John Tyler pushed through Congress a joint resolution authorizing the admission of Texas into the Union. That move provoked tension between the United States and Mexico, a country that felt cheated by the annexation of Texas and that contested American claims regarding Texas's border. Perhaps eager to provoke a war of conquest, President James K. Polk ordered the U.S. Army deep into the contested land. Fighting erupted between U.S. and Mexican soldiers in April 1846, and in early May, Polk asked Congress, in the message printed below, to issue a declaration of war. The message is taken from A Compilation of the Messages and Papers of the Presidents. . ., *ed. James D. Richardson (New York, 1897), 6:2287, 2291–93.*

WASHINGTON, May 11, 1846.
To the Senate and House of Representatives:

The existing state of the relations between the United States and Mexico renders it proper that I should bring the subject to the consideration of Congress. . . .

The Army moved from Corpus Christi on the 11th of March, and on the 28th of that month arrived on the left bank of the Del Norte opposite to Matamoras, where it encamped on a commanding position, which has since been strengthened by the erection of field works. . . .

The Mexican forces at Matamoras assumed a belligerent attitude, and on the 12th of April General Ampudia, then in command, notified General Taylor to break up his camp within twenty-four hours and to retire beyond the Nueces River, and in the event of his failure to comply with these demands announced that arms, and arms alone, must decide the question. . . .

The grievous wrongs perpetrated by Mexico upon our citizens throughout a long period of years remain unredressed, and solemn treaties pledging her public faith for this redress have been disregarded. A government either unable or unwilling to enforce the execution of such treaties fails to perform one of its plainest duties.

. . . Our forbearance has gone to such an extreme as to be mistaken in its character. Had we acted with vigor in repelling the insults and redressing the injuries inflicted by Mexico at the commencement, we should doubtless have escaped all the difficulties in which we are now involved.

Instead of this, however, we have been exerting our best efforts to propitiate her good will. Upon the pretext that Texas, a nation as independent as herself, thought proper to unite its destinies with our own, she has affected to believe that we have severed her rightful territory, and in official proclamations and manifestoes has repeatedly threatened to make war upon us for the purpose of reconquering Texas. In the meantime we have tried every effort at reconciliation. The cup of forbearance had been exhausted even before the recent information from the frontier of the Del Norte. But now, after reiterated menaces, Mexico has passed the boundary of the United States, has invaded our territory and shed American blood upon the American soil. She has proclaimed that hostilities have commenced, and that the two nations are now at war.

As war exists, and, notwithstanding all our efforts to avoid it, exists by the act of Mexico herself, we are called upon by every consideration of duty and patriotism to vindicate with decision the honor, the rights, and the interests of our country. . . .

In further vindication of our rights and defense of our territory, I invoke the prompt action of Congress to recognize the existence of the war, and to place at the disposition of the Executive the means of prosecuting the war with vigor, and thus hastening the restoration of peace.

JAMES K. POLK

Abraham Lincoln
Challenges Polk's Justification for War

The war against Mexico went well for the United States, which eventually occupied Mexico City and forced Mexico to cede approximately one-third of its land. Yet from the earliest days of fighting, many in the United States questioned the legal and moral grounds for conducting what they viewed as an aggressive war of conquest. The following address, delivered by Representative Abraham Lincoln, Whig of Illinois, in Congress on 12 January 1848, raised such concerns. The speech is reprinted from Complete Works of Abraham Lincoln, *ed. John G. Nicolay and John Hay (New York, 1905), 1:329–30, 338–41.*

[T]aking for true all the President states as facts, he falls far short of proving his justification. . . . The President, in his first war message of May, 1846, declares that the soil was ours on which hostilities were commenced by Mexico, and he repeats that declaration almost in the same language in each successive annual message, thus showing that he deems that point a highly essential one. In the importance of that point I entirely agree with the President. To my judgment it is the very point upon which he should be justified, or condemned. . . .

. . . I propose to state my understanding of the true rule for ascertaining the boundary between Texas and Mexico. It is that wherever Texas was exercising jurisdiction was hers; and wherever Mexico was exercising jurisdiction was hers; and that whatever separated the actual exercise of jurisdiction of the one from that of the other was the true boundary between them. . . . The extent of our territory in that region depended not on any treaty-fixed boundary (for no treaty had attempted it), but on revolution. . . .

. . . In my view, just so far as she carried her resolution by obtaining the actual, willing or unwilling, submission of the people, so far the country was hers, and no farther. Now, sir, for the purpose of obtaining the very best evidence as to whether Texas had actually carried her revolution to the place where the hostilities of the present war commenced, let the President answer the interrogatories I proposed, as before mentioned, or some other similar ones. Let him answer fully, fairly, and candidly. . . . And if, so answering, he can show that the soil was ours where the first blood of the war was shed,—that it was not within an inhabited country, or, if within such, that the inhabitants had submitted themselves to the civil authority of Texas or of the United States, and that the same is true of the site of Fort Brown,—then I am with him for his justification. . . . But if he can not or will not do this,— if on any pretense or no pretense he shall refuse or omit it—then I shall be fully convinced of what I more than suspect already—that he is deeply conscious of being in the wrong; that he feels the blood of this war, like the blood of Abel, is crying to Heaven against him; that originally having some strong motive—what, I will not stop now to give my opinion concerning—to involve the two countries in a war, and trusting to escape scrutiny by fixing the public gaze upon the exceeding brightness of military glory,—that attractive rainbow that arises in showers of blood—that serpent's eye that charms to destroy,—he plunged into it, and has swept on and on till, disappointed in his calculation of the ease with which Mexico might be subdued, he now finds himself he knows not where. How like the half-insane mumbling of a fever dream is the whole war part of his late message!

The Expansion of Slavery Justified

The acquisition of vast territory in the southwest raised the question of whether slavery would be permitted to expand there. Representative David Wilmot, a Pennsylvania Democrat, provoked furious debate by proposing in August 1846 a prohibition against slavery in lands acquired in the war. The so-called Wilmot Proviso repeatedly passed the House, where northerners enjoyed a majority, but died in the Senate, where southerners and other Democrats blocked it. The document that follows, an editorial condemning the Wilmot Proviso, first appeared in The United States Magazine and Democratic Review *(October 1847), 21:292.*

All the territory of the Union is the common property of all the states—every member, new or old, of the Union, admitted to partnership under the constitution, has a perfect right to enjoy the territory, which is the common property of all. Some of the territory was acquired by treaty from England—much of it by cession from the older states; yet more by treaties with Indians, and still greater quantities by purchase from Spain and France;—large tracts again by the annexation of Texas—and the present war will add still more to the quantity yet to be entered by citizens of the United States, or of those of any of the countries of Europe that choose to migrate thither. All this land, no matter whence it was derived, belongs to all the states jointly. . . . [N]o citizen of the United States can be debarred from moving thither with his property, and enjoying the liberties guaranteed by the constitution. . . . Any law or regulation which interrupts, limits, delays or postpones the rights of the owner to the immediate command of his service or labor, operates a discharge of the slave from service, and is a violation of the constitution. . . . To set up therefore a pretence that if they adhere to the property they possess, they shall be deprived of their rights in the states to be formed in any acquired territory, is an unprincipled violation of a solemn treaty, an attack upon the constitution, and a gross injustice to the rights of neighboring states. If the constitution is respected, then the rights of no member in the common property can be impaired, because it is possessed of other property distasteful to other members.

The Expansion of Slavery Condemned

Among the most strident supporters of the Wilmot Proviso stood the noted abolitionist Charles Sumner of Massachusetts. In this treatise, written for the Massachusetts legislature in April 1847, Sumner criticizes the war against Mexico on anti-slavery and other grounds. Taken from "Report on the War with Mexico," in Old South Leaflets, *no. 132 (Boston, n.d.), 150–53, 155–56 [separately paginated as 14–17, 19–20].*

It can no longer be doubted that this is a war of conquest. . . .

A war of conquest is bad; but the present war has darker shadows. It is a war for the extension of slavery over a territory which has already been purged, by Mexican authority, from this stain and curse. Fresh markets of human beings are to be established; further opportunities for this hateful traffic are to be opened; the lash of the overseer is to be quickened in new regions; and the wretched slave is to be hurried to unaccustomed fields of toil. It can hardly be believed that now, more than eighteen hundred years since the dawn of the Christian era, a government, professing the law of charity and justice, should be employed in war to extend an institution which exists in defiance of these sacred principles.

It has already been shown that the annexation of Texas was consummated for this purpose. The Mexican war is a continuance, a prolongation, of the same efforts; and the success which crowned the first emboldens the partisans of the latter, who now, as before, profess to extend the area of freedom, while they are establishing a new sphere for slavery. . . . But it is not merely proposed to open new markets for slavery: it is also designed to confirm and fortify the "Slave Power.". . . Regarding it as a war to strengthen the "Slave Power," we are conducted to a natural conclusion, that it is virtually, and in its consequences, a war against the free States of the Union. . . . Nor should we be indifferent to the enormous expenditures which have already been lavished upon the war, and the accumulating debt which will hold in mortgage the future resources of the country. It is impossible to estimate the exact amount of these. At this moment the cost of the war cannot be less than seventy millions. It may be a hundred millions.

This sum is so vast as to be beyond easy comprehension. It may be estimated, partly, by reference to the cost of other objects of interest. It is far more than all the funds for common schools throughout the United States. It is ample for the endowment of three or more institutions like Harvard College in every State. It would plant churches in all the neglected valleys of the land. It would bind and interlace every part of the country by new railroads. It would make our broad and rude soil blossom like a garden. . . .

. . . The war is a crime, and all who have partaken in the blood of its well-fought fields have aided in its perpetration. It is a principle of military law that the soldier shall not question the orders of his superior. If this shall exonerate the army from blame, it will be only to press with accumulated weight upon the government, which has set in motion this terrible and irresponsible machine.

Mormon Migration

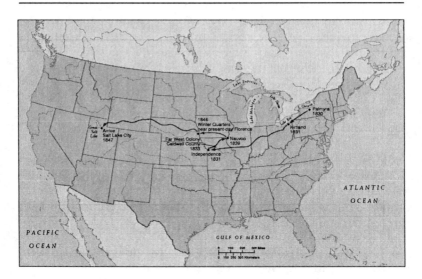

Reprinted with the permission of Prentice Hall from Out of Many: A History of the American People, *Third Edition, by John Mack Faragher, Mari Jo Buhle, Daniel Czitrom, and Susan H. Armitage. Copyright © 2000 by Prentice-Hall, Inc.*

Territory Added to U.S., 1845-53

Reprinted with the permission of Prentice Hall from Out of Many: A
History of the American People, *Third Edition, by John Mack
Faragher, Mari Jo Buhle, Daniel Czitrom, and Susan H. Armitage.
Copyright © 2000 by Prentice-Hall, Inc.*

Practice DBQ

Evaluate the main arguments in favor of and against American territorial expansion in the 1840s and explain why the nation continued to expand geographically at this time.

Remember that you should use your knowledge of American history and the primary sources in answering the Document-Based Question. You should take about forty-five minutes to complete your response.

Recommended Web Sites

http://www.yale.edu/lawweb/avalon/monroe.htm
See the text of President James Monroe's address to Congress; his explanation of America's foreign policy interests became known as the Monroe Doctrine.

http://www.mtholyoke.edu/acad/intrel/osulliva.htm
John O'Sullivan's article explaining America's destiny to move west.

http://www.dmwv.org/mexwar/polk.htm
President James K. Polk's address to Congress asking for declaration of war against Mexico.

http://www.pbs.org/weta/thewest/resources/archives/index.htm
Material from a PBS documentary on the West. This site has many interesting primary sources.

http://www.learner.org/biographyofamerica/prog07/feature/
Good interactive map of growth of railroads, canals, and roads 1830-1860.

From Artisans to Factory Hands: The Beginnings of an Industrial Society

Warren R. Van Tine

INTRODUCTION

The first half of the nineteenth century witnessed the "take-off" stage of industrialism in America. Efforts to expand production were stimulated by improvements in transportation—better roads, new canals, scheduled shipping, and the rise of the railroad—that enabled an enterprising producer to sell to an expanded market. Technological improvements, like Eli Whitney's cotton gin and his work on techniques to make interchangeable parts for muskets helped increase production. But the "take-off" stage of industrialism was not primarily driven by the invention of new machines. Rather, the most important causes of the initial increase in production were a reorganization of how work was done and a concomitant restructuring of the habits and culture of the people performing that work. The reorganization of work was achieved by pulling the various tasks involved in making a product away from their diverse locations and putting them under a single roof, a "manufactory." The restructuring of values and culture was a more subtle enterprise that activated many of the social reform and religious movements of the antebellum years. At the time of the Civil War, the United States was still an overwhelmingly agrarian nation, yet almost all observers agreed that industrialism and the cultural forces it carried with it were the wave of the future.

TRANSITION TO INDUSTRIAL DISCIPLINE

The documents that follow present various aspects of the transition that occurred in working-class life and work during the early stages of industrialism. The passage about ship carpenters captures the libertine work ethic of these early artisans. The letter from "A Mechanic" points out how lifestyles were restructured as a result of the transportation revolution. Alonzo Lewis' poem on Election Day comments on the abolition of a preindustrial celebration, while the two sets of work regulations at the end of this section lay out the new behavior standards expected of workers in the industrial age. Collectively, these documents hint at a fundamental transition in American culture in the decades prior to the Civil War. To native-born artisans this transition was sharply apparent, but the thousands of immigrating laborers from Great Britain put conditions in industrializing America into a different context. The last two documents present the impressions of an English and an Irish traveller to America, and suggest why so many Europeans thought life in the United States would be so much better.

A Ship Carpenter's Day

The syncopated nature of work and leisure in preindustrial worklife, both over time and during a specific day, was captured by Richard Trevellick in the 1830s. He clearly conveys a sense of work-culture among New

From *Looking for America*, Second Edition, Volume 1 by Stanley I. Kutler. Copyright © 1979, 1976 by Stanley I. Kutler. Reprinted by permission of W. W. Norton & Company, Inc.

York ship carpenters. This document is taken from Looking for America: The People's History, *ed. Stanley I. Kutler, 2d ed. (New York, 1979), 1:267–68, 270.*

Everywhere, from the government ship-yards down to the ten-ton sloop set up in the woods miles from any place, the rule holds good. Hurrah! hurry and hiring men to-day; to-morrow, or day after, or next week, the place is as quiet as a grave-yard; the crisis is passed, hurry is over, the craft launched and gone, and so all the craftsmen—scattered in as many directions, perhaps, as there are men, in search of some other three-weeks' job.

In some four or five of our larger cities ship-work is something more continuous and reliable; but even they are by no means exempt from depressions and sudden fluctuations; and whenever the "slack time" comes if the ship-carpenter, caulker, joiner, etc., is not absolutely discharged, his wages are reduced until he finds himself wondering "what he will do with it," his remuneration, at the highest figure, being no greater than that of some half a dozen other classes of mechanics, whose employment is constant and always under shelter, so that whatever time they may lose is voluntary. . . .

As the order of labor in those days was to fall to in the morning at the first glance the bosses could catch at a sunbeam gilding the tallest spire in sight,—there being no steeple in sight from the "Hook," bosses used to catch their matin sunbeams from the vane of the 170-foot Liberty-pole over in Grand street, below Lewis,—the stretch during the summer solstice, from "commencement" to twelve o'clock, was rather a long and tedious one. It would have been far more tedious but for an indulgence that custom had made as much of a necessity in a New York ship-yard as a grind-stone.

In our yard, at half-past eight A.M., Aunt Arlie McVane, a clever, kind-hearted but awfully uncouth, rough sample of the "Ould Sod," would make her welcome appearance in the yard with her two great baskets, stowed and checked off with crullers, doughnuts, ginger-bread, turnovers, pies, and a variety of sweet cookies and cakes; and from the time Aunt Arlie's baskets came in sight until every man and boy, bosses and all, in the yard, had been supplied, always at one cent apiece for any article in the cargo, the pie, cake and cookie trade was a brisk one. Aunt Arlie would usually make the round of the yard and supply all hands in about an hour, bringing the forenoon up to half-past nine, and giving us from ten to fifteen minutes' breathing spell during lunch; no one ever hurried during "cake-time."

After this was over we would fall to again, until interrupted by Johnnie Gogean, the English candy-man, who came in always about half-past ten, with his great board, the size of a medium extension dining-table, slung before him, covered with all sorts of "stick," and several of sticky, candy, in one-cent lots. Bosses, boys and men—all hands, everybody—invested one to three cents in Johnnie's sweet wares, and another ten or fifteen minutes is spent in consuming it. Johnnie usually sailed out with a bare board about eleven o'clock, at which time there was a general sailing out of the yard and into convenient grog-shops after whiskey; only we had four or five men among us, and one apprentice—not quite a year my senior—who used to sail out pretty regularly ten times a day on an average; two that went for whiskey only when some one invited them to drink, being too mean to treat themselves; and two more who never went at all.

In the afternoon, about half-past three, we had a cake-lunch, supplied by Uncle Jack Grider, an old, crippled, superannuated ship-carpenter. No one else was ever allowed to come in competition with our caterers. Let a foreign candy-board or cake-basket make their appearance inside of the gates of our yard, and they would get chipped out of that directly.

At about five o'clock P.M., always, Johnnie used to put in his second appearance; and then, having expended money in another stick or two of candy, and ten minutes or so in its consumption, we were ready to drive away again till sun-down; then off home to supper.

Railroads and Competition

The following letter from "A Mechanic" in Georgia explains how the transportation revolution widened market opportunities for manufacturers and increased the competitive pressures on local artisans. This letter is taken from A Documentary History of American Industrial Society, *ed. John R. Commons et al. (Cleveland, 1910), 2:336–37.*

Brother Mechanics of Georgia, and Especially of our own Village: The Mechanics of all kinds in this country are injured by rail roads to some extent. They are brought single handed to compete with those large manufacturing establishments in the northern States and foreign countries, where labor is worth comparatively nothing, brought in opposition by the aid of steam and the rail roads as it were in your own village, by the transportation of the manufactured articles of all kinds, and sold at your own shop doors at reduced prices by your own merchants, and bought by your own farmers, from whom you expected patronage. Is not this one of the main causes why your villages are not flourishing, the houses vacant, and in a dilapidated condition, your academies destitute of teachers, or if teachers, destitute of pupils? It certainly is one of the main causes why Mechanics are reduced to poverty, not being able to build up our towns and cities or to educate their children so as to make them respectable members of society. Brother mechanics, this is not as it should be—then rouse up from your lethargy, go drooped down and depressed no longer, come forth in your might and power, and at once, as it were, you will be able to correct the evil. —You should form yourselves into large and permanent manufacturing companies. With your skill and enterprise you may soon rear up in your midst, manufacturing establishments of various kinds to manufacture those very articles that afford a considerable item in the commerce of the country, make your towns and villages soon become flourishing, affording a great market for surplus products, raised by the farmers in our own midst—and as all classes will feel the benefit in a short time it will be but a little while before your business will be profitable to yourselves and the country in which you live. I might be asked to suggest some plan to give the above suggestions a permanent and practical notice to the community at large. One that I would mention is that it should be the business of every mechanic of every branch of business, to apply himself closely to his business. Let that be his daily employment, instead of, as is too often the case, quitting his shop, taking the streets, becoming a street politician, a dandy, or a drunkard. Remedy those three evils and the work is half accomplished.

A MECHANIC.

The Days of Old 'Lection Are Over

As part of the drive to do away with preindustrial practices, in 1831 the Massachusetts legislature abolished Election Day's status as a holiday. In the following poem, Alonzo Lewis, a Lynn resident, bemoans the loss of this once joyous occasion. This poem was reprinted in Paul Faler, "Cultural Aspects of the Industrial Revolution: Lynn, Massachusetts, Shoemakers and Industrial Morality, 1826–1860," Labor History *15 (1974): 382.*

And is Election Day no more?
Good old 'Lection . . .
No more shall we go up
To see "Old Willis!"
He has hung up his fiddle
On the last peg.
The days of old 'Lection are over.
The glorious days of "Landee John!"
When "Gid" used to hustle coppers,
And the niggers play "paw-paw"
On Boston Common.
No more shall we eat 'Lection Cake,
Or drink muddy beer,
Misnomered "ale,"
At "Old Bly's."
The days of dancing "Suke" are done,
And fat "Bet" shall shake her jolly sides no more
To the merry winding about
Of linked sweetness, long drawn out,
From old "Pompey's fiddle!"
No more shall "the Governor"
Sit in his great arm-chair,
To encounter the stare
Of the idle mixed multitude,

"Black spirits and white,
Blue spirits and gray,"
Barefoot and booted,
Maudlin and merry.
Yes, 'Lection is done
With all its paraphernalia
Of cocked-up hats and fun.

Regulations Governing Workers' Conduct at the Springfield Armory

As early manufacturers brought workers together under their immediate supervision, they issued rules to control their employees' behavior. The following regulations were enforced beginning in 1816 at the Springfield (Massachusetts) Armory, one of the earliest industrial establishments. This document was reproduced in Christopher S. Duckworth, "Man, Manpower, and Machines at the Springfield Armory: The Superintendency of Roswell Lee, 1815–1833" (M. A. thesis, The Ohio State University, 1975), 50–52.

Regulations Governing Workers' Conduct
Adopted 8 March, 1816

The amount of the value of all public property or property located on lands belonging to the United States (personal or moveable property owned by the workmen or other individuals excepted) that is wantonly maliciously or carelessly wasted injured or destroyed will be deducted from the pay of the person so offending. No scuffling playing of Ball or other proceedings that have a tendency to impede the regular advancement and progress of the work will be suffered in the Public work shops nor within thirty rods of the same.

No fighting will be allowed or tolerated among the workmen.

No indecent or unnecessary noise will be suffered in or about the shops.

The workmen employed in the Armory are hereby cautioned against riotous and tumultous conduct and every person who shall begin, excite, or join, in any mutinous, riotous or seditious, conduct against the regulations of the Armory, or shall oppose the officers, when in the execution of their duty, or shall wilfully refuse to observe the Lawful directions of the Officers of the Armory will be prosecuted before the United States Court and dismissed from the Armory.

All combinations against the Officers or regulations of the Armory will be noticed by an immediate reduction of wages of all concerned, or in such other manner as in the opinion of the Superintendent, circumstances may require—Except for improper conduct the workmen will not be dismissed until thirty days after notice is given, and the same notice as to time is required from the workmen to be given to the Superintendent or Master Armorer previous to their leaving work in the Armory, that is, one month's labor will be expected after such notice is given—A workman will be considered as having forfeited his place in the Armory by a violation of any of the foregoing regulations or by absenting himself from the Public works for more than two days in succession or more than four days in a month without the knowledge and approbation of the Superintendent or Master Armorer or at the Water Shops of the Foreman of the Shop where the person wishing to be absent is employed—

From and after the 15th day of April 1816 no Rum, Gin, Brandy, Whiskey, or ardent Spirits of any kind will be suffered to be carried or drunk in or about the public work shops at this place, and the Master Armorer, Assistants, Foremen and Inspectors are directed to see that this regulation is strictly adhered to.

In the absence of the Superintendent the duties of that office will devolve upon the Master Armorer.

Factory Regulations in Lowell

The regulations imposed by the Hamilton Manufacturing Company of Lowell, Massachusetts went beyond controlling behavior on the shop floor and invaded the worker's personal life. The following document is from A Documentary History of American Industrial Society, *ed. John R. Commons et al. (Cleveland, 1910), 7:135–36.*

REGULATIONS TO BE OBSERVED by all persons employed in the factories of the Hamilton Manufacturing Company. The overseers are to be always in their rooms at the starting of the mill, and not absent unnecessarily during working hours. They are to see that all those employed in their rooms, are in their places in due season, and keep a correct account of their time and work. They may grant leave of absence to those employed under them, when they have spare hands to supply their places, and not otherwise, except in cases of absolute necessity.

All persons in the employ of the Hamilton Manufacturing Company, are to observe the regulations of the room where they are employed. They are not to be absent from their work without the consent of the overseer, except in cases of sickness, and then they are to send him word of the cause of their absence. They are to board in one of the houses of the company and give information at the counting room, where they board, when they begin, or, whenever they change their boarding place; and are to observe the regulations of their boarding-house.

Those intending to leave the employment of the company, are to give at least two weeks' notice thereof to their overseer.

All persons entering into the employment of the company, are considered as engaged for twelve months, and those who leave sooner, or do not comply with all these regulations, will not be entitled to a regular discharge.

The company will not employ any one who is habitually absent from public worship on the Sabbath, or known to be guilty of immorality.

A physician will attend once in every month at the counting-room, to vaccinate all who may need it, free of expense.

Any one who shall take from the mills or the yard, any yarn, cloth or other article belonging to the company, will be considered guilty of stealing and be liable to prosecution.

Payment will be made monthly, including board and wages. The accounts will be made up to the last Saturday but one in every month, and paid in the course of the following week.

These regulations are considered part of the contract, with which all persons entering into the employment of the Hamilton Manufacturing Company, engage to comply.

JOHN AVERY, Agent.

Two Foreign Travellers' Observations

While American-born artisans were troubled by the changes they experienced in the workplace and community, European-born travelers to America saw the industrial transformation in a different light. In the following documents, an Englishman in 1843 and an Irishman in 1850 offer diverse observations about working-class life in America as compared to their homelands. Taken from A Documentary History of the American Industrial Society, *ed. John R. Commons et al. (Cleveland, 1910), 7:47–56, 71–73, 75–76.*

[An Englishman's View]

It is much easier to obtain employment, at present, in the United States than in England; but in this respect they are getting into a worse and worse condition. The manufacturers, in the East, have introduced all our improvements in machinery, (and the effects are the same as in this country) they are making very large quantities of goods; competition is increasing, prices are very much reduced, and the wages of labour, generally, throughout the States and Canada, have been reduced from thirty to fifty per cent within the last four years, and wages are still reducing in some parts of the country, in spite of their trades' unions and democratic institutions; and, if competition continue, no parties can prevent wages from falling as low there as they are in England, and this within a comparatively short period. Wages in America are not much higher, even now, than they are with us. Agricultural labourers can be hired, in Illinois and other states, for from eight to twelve dollars per month. Smiths and mechanics for from twelve to eighteen dollars per month, with board. The boarding of labourers of all kinds is almost universal in the small towns and villages in the agricultural districts. . . .

The price of fuel, and the rents of houses for labourers are very high in all the eastern states; food is also much higher there than in the west. It is highest at Boston and New York, but even there, food is from 25 to 50 per cent cheaper than in Liverpool. Rents are high in all parts of the Union, and clothing is higher than it is with us. Wood fuel can be had for merely the expense of cutting and preparing in most parts of the west. . . .

One of the greatest evils the working classes have to contend with in the United States and in Canada, for it is generally practised in both countries, is the abominable cheating truck system, which is carried on with more barefaced impudence there, and to a greater extent than it ever was practised in this country. The following is a verbatim copy of a printed notice given by Ben. Cozzens, a large manufacturer, who has two large cotton factories and a print work, and employs from a thousand to fifteen hundred pair of hands, at Crompton mills in Rhode Island. Single men at board, who cannot take goods, have ten per cent deducted from their wages in lieu of it.

Notice. Those employed at these mills and works will take notice, that a store is kept for their accommodation, where they can purchase the best of goods at fair prices, and it is expected that all will draw their goods from said store. Those who do not are informed, that there are plenty of others who would be glad to take their places at less wages.   Benj. Cozzens.

Crompton Mills, February, 1843.

One of the printed notices, from which this was copied, was put into my hands by a man who lately worked for Benjamin Cozzens, and who has returned home, tired of America, in the Roscius. Five colliers returned home by the same vessel, who had been working at Pittsville, in Pennsylvania, where the same vile truck system is carried on to the greatest extent. They declared that when their American wages were turned into cash, they could earn as much, and were as well off, in their own country. I know the general prevalence of this system, by information from masters as well as men. The average of loss to the workmen by this system is not less than twenty-five per cent of their wages, and in many cases it is attended with a loss of fifty per cent. When masters have no shops of their own, they give notes to the men to get their goods at other shops, who supply them with inferior articles at high prices, and out of the money the workmen are cheated of, they allow a per centage to the master. In many places the shopkeepers will not give flour and groceries for these notes; they tell them these are cash articles only, in which case the men are compelled to take other goods which they do not want, and then have to submit to a still greater loss in disposing of them for cash to get absolute necessaries. . . .

. . . In judging of their condition, you must take into account the length and severity of their winters, and the excessive heat of their summers, in the northern states and in Canada. Their winters commence in November, and continue till the end of April—about six months in the year—during which period all building operations, and all agricultural employments, except the felling of timber and preparing fuel, are suspended; and, being all frozen up, navigation on their rivers and canals, and all employments dependent on these, are stopped; and many other employments, depending on water power, are also stopped; the cold is so excessive that the thermometer is frequently twenty degrees below zero; they are obliged to keep large fires in their dwellings, and to have a large quantity of extra warm clothing to prevent them from perishing; it is often dangerous to go out of doors for any length of time, in winter, without completely covering every part of the body; parties sometimes have their nose, or some other part of their face, frozen, without being aware of it themselves; a friend meets them, and tells them that they are frozen, the remedy is immediately to rub the part affected with snow, which restores it; but many perish from cold, particularly the blacks in Canada. As goods cannot be brought to the ports, commerce is also in a great degree prevented. The consequence is, that unless workmen get good wages and plenty of work in summer, to enable them to lay in a good supply for winter; their condition is and must be much more wretched than the labourers in England. Indeed, for several winters past, and especially last winter, great numbers out of employment in Boston, Salem, Providence, New York, and other places, were supplied with soup, bread, fuel, and other articles, by charitable contributions. . . .

In the middle of summer, on the contrary, the weather is so excessively hot, (frequently ninety to a hundred degrees), that it is very difficult to do a day's work at hard labour, beside which, in the western states, you are much annoyed by the bite of mosquitoes, and, in those parts, fever and ague are very prevalent in summer. . . .

I was talking with some of the workmen, spinners, in the largest jean manufactory in Steubenville, in the state of Ohio, who were telling me of the recent reductions in their wages, and of the rascally truck system, which is universally practised in that town and neighborhood—the workmen are generally paid by notes on the shops, by which they lose at least 25 per cent, in price and quality; but, they are frequently paid in pieces of jean of their own make, charged at high prices, by which they often lose 50 per cent, which reduces their actual wages to about 2s. per day, English money. I asked why they submitted to these impositions, why they did not leave it and go to the land, &c. They replied—"The land in Ohio is dear, generally, and we could not travel to the west without money, and we cannot save money; it is as much as we can do to provide our families with necessaries. We should want money to travel, then money would be wanted to buy the land, to buy agricultural implements, to buy seed, and then we should want more to support us till we could dispose of part of our crops, and we have no money at all. But, suppose we had all these means, we know nothing about the cultivation of land—we have all our lives worked in a factory, and know no other employment, and how is it likely that we should succeed? besides which, we have always been used to live in a town, where we can get what little things we want if we have money, and it is only those who have lived in the wilderness, who know what the horrors of a wilderness-life are."

From what has been said it must be evident to our readers: First. That the wages of labour are everywhere falling in the United States and in Canada, and that the condition of the working population is getting worse and worse, in spite of their high protective duties upon foreign goods, and every other means they have adopted to prevent these reductions.

Second. That the vile truck system is carried on in these countries to a greater extent than it was ever practised in our own, in spite of annual parliaments, universal suffrage, and vote by ballot.

Third. That going upon the land, on the most favourable terms, under a system of society based upon competition, would afford no remedy for these evils, but would in the end only increase them, even though there were neither rent, tithes, nor taxes to be paid.

Fourth. That American labourers, being necessarily idle nearly half the year, during the winter, ought to receive double our English wages in summer, to place them on equal terms with English labourers, which is not the case, as their wages are nominally very little higher than they are here. The only advantages they have are more employment, freedom from taxes, and the cheapness of provisions. But we have seen that even the cheapness of food is a great injury to the mass of the people, the agricultural population.

Fifth. That the causes of those evils are the same in America as in England, the vast extension of scientific and mechanical power, and the consequent great increase of manufactured goods, and the great and rapid extension of agricultural operations; by which means an immense surplus is produced, whilst competition reduces everything to so low a price that no parties are able to get a remuneration for producing them; and that all that is wanted, either in America or in England, is, rational arrangements to distribute the wealth produced in a just and equitable manner for the benefit of all classes.

[An Irishman's View]

Nor do they content themselves with learning one trade only. Most young mechanics learn two trades, and that in half the time usually devoted to acquire trades in Ireland; two to three years is about the measure of time devoted to the study of a mechanical branch in America. They labour hard in the day, and they attend all kinds of lectures, instruction, and amusements in the evening. The young girls who work in factories, or at trades in their own homes, pay superior teachers for instruction in the light and more elegant female accomplishments, such as singing, music, dancing, drawing and languages.

The necessity imposed upon every one to obtain by his or her own exertions a living, begets that industry which pervades every American family. Every member of the family will do something to contribute to the family commonwealth: though the father may hold a public office, the boys are ready and willing to do any work which they know how to do to obtain money. . . .

A great share of the light manufacture of America, is done by women in the farm-houses, especially in the New England states. For instance, straw bonnets. There are large straw bonnet establishments in New York and Boston, which have their agents continually travelling among the farm-houses. This agent drives a sort of van or omnibus, and brings round bunches of straw plait, and models of bonnets of the newest fashion. These he leaves with the farmers' wives and daughters, all round the country, who work up into bonnets, according to the peculiar model, the plait so left. In due season the agent returns with some more plait, and distributes it to the straw-sewers as before, and receives up the bonnets, for the making of which he pays. All the females of an entire district, including the doctors' and ministers' wives, are engaged in this work. . . . Nor is it all work and no play with these republicans. On the contrary, the boys and girls, of a family have plenty of money of their own saving, and no people of the world enjoy more public amusement. Lectures, concerts, balls, pictorial exhibitions, theatricals, circuses, are to be met with in every village and hamlet. Every swarming village has its reading room and "lyceum," in which a course of public lectures is delivered during the winter. Those lectures embrace all that is interesting to the people, from the constitution of man to that of steam engines. The people are passionately fond of music and dancing, and all such amusements. They dress gaily, and wear out their clothes very fast; but they have a perpetual income from their industry, on which they rely in full confidence to replenish their wardrobes and their pockets. They keep their persons very neat, very cleanly, and study much the art of dress. I think they are the best dressed population in the world, though it must be admitted that streaks of absurdity are sometimes visible in their sumptual economy. . .

The food of the American farmer, mechanic, or labourer, is the best I believe enjoyed by any similar classes in the whole world. At every meal there is meat, or fish, or both; indeed, I think the women, children, and sedentary classes, eat too much meat for their own good health. However, it is an error on the right side, easily cured when discovered. The breakfast of the common people is made up of coffee or tea, fish meat, butter, bread, potatoes, all on the table. Dinner: meat and fish, potatoes, bread, pies made of apples or berries of all sorts, indian pudding. Supper: tea, meat, bread, hot cakes, &c.

This kind of diet, or "board," with lodging and washing, can be had in the "mechanics' boarding houses" in any of the cities of America (except those in the south) at two and a half dollars a week (11s. British) for men, and one dollar and a half (6s. 6d. British) for women. In the western states the same board and lodging can be had by the same classes for two dollars (8s. 6d. British) a week for men, and one dollar for women. In the southern cities board is nearly double these rates.

From all these causes the value of common manual labour is higher in the United States than in any other part of the world. The average value of a common uneducated labourer is 80 cents (3s. 4d.) a day. Of educated or mechanical labour, 125 to 200 cents (5s. to 8s.) a day; of female labour, 40 cents (1s. 8d.) a day. Against meat, flour, vegetables, and groceries at one-third less than they rate in Great Britain and Ireland; against clothing, house rent and fuel, at about equal; against public taxes at about three-fourths less; and a certainty of employment, and the facility of acquiring houses and lands, and education for children, a hundred to one greater. The farther you penetrate into the country, Patrick, the higher in general will you find the value of labour, and the cheaper the price of all kinds of living.

Urban Population, 1820 and 1860

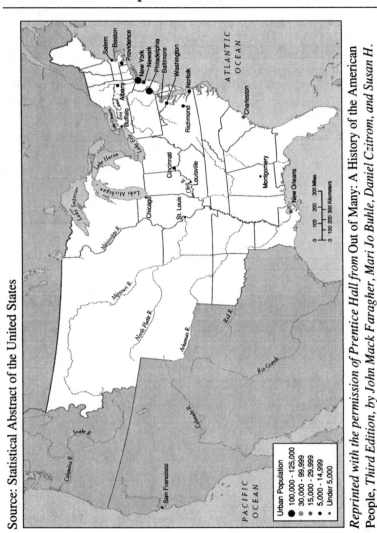

Source: Statistical Abstract of the United States

Reprinted with the permission of Prentice Hall from Out of Many: A History of the American People, Third Edition, by John Mack Faragher, Mari Jo Buhle, Daniel Czitrom, and Susan H. Armitage. Copyright © 2000 by Prentice-Hall, Inc.

Source: Statistical Abstract of the United States

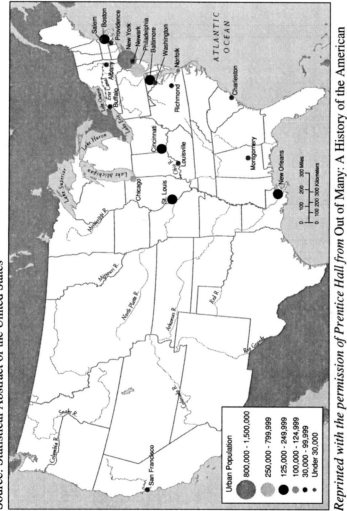

Reprinted with the permission of Prentice Hall from Out of Many: A History of the American People, Third Edition, by John Mack Faragher, Mari Jo Buhle, Daniel Czitrom, and Susan H. Armitage. Copyright © 2000 by Prentice-Hall, Inc.

Decreasing Travel Times

Impact of the
Transportation Revolution
on Traveling Time

Route	1800	1830	1860
New York to Philadelphia	2 days	1 day	Less than 1 day
New York to Charleston	More than 1 week	5 days	2 days
New York to Chicago	6 weeks	3 weeks	2 days
New York to New Orleans	4 weeks	2 weeks	6 days

Reprinted with the permission of Prentice Hall from The American
Journey: A History of the United States, *Second Edition, by David
Goldfield, Carl Abbott, Virginia DeJohn Anderson, Jo Ann E.
Argersinger, Peter H. Argersinger, William L. Barney, and Robert M.
Weir. Copyright © 2001 by Prentice-Hall, Inc.*

Practice DBQ

How did Americans' everyday lives change as a result of industrialization in the early nineteenth century?

*Remember that you should use your knowledge of American history and
the primary sources in answering the Document-Based Question. You
should take about forty-five minutes to complete your response.*

Recommended Web Sites

http://www.kentlaw.edu/ilhs/lowell.html
Copies of work regulations in the 1840s. Includes rules for
workers at the textile mills in Lowell, Massachusetts, description
of factory work, and an investigation into labor conditions.

http://www.uwp.edu/academic/history/hist314/vmtedl/
lowell.htm
Good images of the textile mills at Lowell.

http://applebutter.freeservers.com/worker/
Evidence of effects of working in a factory. The documents here
are from English factories, but they were reprinted in the United
States in the beginning of the nineteenth century. Note that other
countries were going through industrialization at the same time
as the United States.

http://www.library.csi.cuny.edu/dept/americanstudies/
lavender/graphics/spinsong.jpg
Sheet music of a song sung by "mill girls" who worked at
Lowell.

http://www.library.csi.cuny.edu/dept/americanstudies/
lavender/lowetext.html#transcript
Excerpt from a newspaper article about a Lowell strike. Also
includes a labor song and a poem from the mill workers.

http://www.library.csi.cuny.edu/dept/americanstudies/
lavender/graphics/ttable.jpg
The daily schedule for Lowell girls. Note the regimentation of
life at the textile factory.

 http://www.fordham.edu/halsall/mod/robinson-lowell.html
First-hand account of a woman who worked at Lowell.

http://www.albany.edu/faculty/gz580/His316/
WeekintheMill.html
Contemporary essay about working in Lowell.

The Political Crisis
of the 1850s

Tyler Anbinder

INTRODUCTION

Most students of America's past realize that the Civil War marked a major turning point in the nation's history. But we often forget that the ultimate cause of the war was the inability of politicians to find a means of compromising conflicting views concerning slavery and its extension. An understanding of the causes and consequences of the political crisis of the 1850s is thus a prerequisite to an appreciation of the origins of the "War Between the States."

There were four crucial elements in the political crisis that led to the Civil War. First, the "party system" pitting Democrats against Whigs collapsed. Second, the strongest new party to emerge in the wake of this collapse—the Republican party—was a sectional one that drew nearly all its support from non-slave states. Third, the Republicans by 1858 captured control of the more conservative Northern states by moderating and expanding their platform to include issues other than slavery. Finally, the Republican success exacerbated the already growing polarization between North and South, making it no longer possible for Americans to compromise their differences concerning the slavery extension issue. American statesmen had once prided themselves on their ability to forge compromises on the question of involuntary servitude. In 1787, 1820, and 1850, national leaders had averted crises by crafting compromises on slavery supported by a majority of Americans. This last compromise had been brokered primarily through the efforts of two Whigs—Senator Henry Clay of Kentucky and President Millard Fillmore of New York—and one Democrat, Stephen A. Douglas of Illinois. After 1850, however, consensus on the slavery issue became impossible. Nothing better reflects the increasing divisions over slavery than the Kansas-

Nebraska Act of 1854. This law repealed the Missouri Compromise of 1820 by allowing involuntary servitude in federal territories where it had previously been banned, if their white residents approved. The law's most important Northern supporters, Douglas and President Franklin Pierce of New Hampshire, were surprised at the breadth of bitter protest generated in the North by the Kansas-Nebraska Act. The Kansas-Nebraska Act made future sectional compromise impossible because in its wake the old parties that had forged previous compromises became weaker (in the case of the Democrats) or died away (in the case of the Whigs). The new parties that emerged—the Know Nothings and the Republicans—evinced far less interest in making compromises. Thus, the destruction of what political scientists call the "second American party system" (that pitting Whigs against Democrats) was the first crucial event of the 1850s that led the nation toward civil war.

Initially, it was not clear whether the Know Nothings or the Republicans would become the main challenger to the Democratic party. The Know Nothings (so called because they claimed to "know nothing" about their initially secret party) believed that their mixture of anti-immigrant, anti-Catholic, anti-liquor, and moderate anti-slavery rhetoric gave them the broad appeal that could sweep them to the White House. Record levels of immigration in the decade after the onset of the potato famine in Ireland profoundly changed the fabric of American society. Cities became more crowded and dirty, and poverty and crime increased dramatically as the immigrants flooded in. Even rural residents in districts that had once received few immigrants now found significant numbers of newcomers in their midst. Because most of the immigrants were Catholics, old political controversies revived concerning whether or not public schools could require the reading of the Protestant King James Bible and whether Catholics should be allowed to send their children to parochial schools at taxpayer expense. Natives also believed that immigrants were responsible for increasing public drunkenness in the United States, especially on Sundays, and that the failure of politicians to enact liquor prohibition laws stemmed from their desire to placate new immigrant voters. Finally, Know Nothings capitalized on significant resentment among many who believed that the Irish immigrants' support of slavery and the Democratic party had made the Kansas-Nebraska Act possible. All these factors enabled the Know Nothings or coalitions led by them to carry many state-wide and mayoral elections in 1854 and 1855.

Republicans at first fared poorly in contests against the Know Nothings. But they were convinced that voters would eventually conclude that Catholics and immigrants posed less of a threat to the United States than did the possible spread of slavery. The Republicans argued that slavery degraded and demeaned the work of Northern free laborers and hurt them financially as well. Events such as the "caning" of anti-slavery Senator Charles Sumner of Massachusetts by a South Carolina colleague and the destruction of the anti-slavery stronghold of Lawrence, Kansas by pro-slavery Missourians (both in May 1856) convinced growing numbers of Northerners that an expanding "Slave Power" would stop at nothing to control the federal government, spread slavery, and stifle debate on the issue. These shocking events drew many previously hesitant Northerners into the Republican ranks. Republicans at this point were still relatively weak, however. In the presidential election of 1856, Democrat James Buchanan of Pennsylvania was the easy victor. But of greater long term importance was that the Republicans far out-polled the Know Nothings, dooming the nativist party to rapid extinction. The second key event of the political crisis of the 1850s—the establishment of the sectional, anti-slavery Republican party as the primary competitor to the Democrats—had been achieved.

Although Republican candidates fared well in 1856 in New England and the upper Midwest, they could not hope to win a presidential election or control Congress unless they did better in more moderate free states such as Illinois, Indiana, Pennsylvania, and New Jersey. Some Republicans believed that they should endorse facets of the Know Nothing agenda (such as restrictions on immigrant voting) to win support in these states. Others argued that such a strategy would alienate the party's immigrant adherents (especially Protestant Germans in the Midwest). Some advised that the way to increase Republican strength in the lower

North was to moderate the party's heated anti-slavery rhetoric and broaden its platform to include issues such as a higher tariff on imports, a stance popular (especially after the financial panic of 1857) with many of the ex-Whigs the Republicans sought to attract. Historians disagree about which of these factors played the most important role in increasing Republican strength after 1856. But there can be no doubt that the Republicans' control of the "lower North" by the end of 1858 represents the third important step in the political crisis that led to the Civil War.

The fourth and final key aspect of the political crisis of the 1850s was the increasing polarization between North and South, which destroyed what little chance remained for compromise on slavery and a de-escalation of section tensions. The Supreme Court's 1857 decision in Dred Scott v. Sanford outraged Northerners by declaring that Congress had no right to ban slavery from a territory. It also made compromise less likely by forbidding the re-establishment of the Missouri Compromise line, the only apparent middle ground between Republicans calling for no more slave states and Southerners who believed they should be permitted to bring their "property" to any federal territory. Continuing fighting (both physical and political) in Kansas over whether to admit that territory as a slave state (as Buchanan and all Southerners desired) or with a free-state constitution (as Douglas and most other Northerners preferred) further enflamed sectional hostility. John Brown's 1859 attempt to incite a slave rebellion with a raid on the federal arsenal at Harpers Ferry, Virginia was also vitally important. It convinced Southerners that despite Republican promises not to interfere with slavery where it already existed, Northerners would stop at nothing to destroy slavery throughout the republic.

The political crisis of the 1850s thus lay at the heart of the events that led to the Civil War. The destruction of the "second party system" removed the old structure that had forged the compromises of the past. The emergence of the Republican party as the main competitor to the Democrats meant that slavery would become a central issue of political debate. The Republicans' control of nearly every Northern state by 1858 convinced them that their dream of *"no more slave states"* might become a reality, while Southerners were equally certain that the **Dred Scott** decision would make such a policy impossible to enforce by allowing slavery to take root in each territory before statehood. By 1860, most politicians were either unwilling or unable to fight this polarization of opinion between the sections. These conditions made the Republican Abraham Lincoln's victory in the presidential contest of 1860, the resulting secession of most slave states, and the civil war that followed, all but inevitable.

DOCUMENTING THE POLITICAL CRISIS OF THE 1850s

The political crisis of the 1850s was primarily a Northern phenomenon. It was Northern voters' rejection of the Whig party and embrace of the Know Nothings that caused the collapse of the second party system that had pitted Whigs against Democrats. Likewise, Republican party success at wooing the Northern electorate allowed it to replace the Whigs as the nation's second major party, and its success electing Lincoln in 1860 precipitated the secession of eleven southern states that started the Civil War. As previously mentioned, these were two of the key elements in the political crisis that led to the Civil War. The following documents show how and why these events took place. The documents reflect the variety of Northern political opinion, party leaders' beliefs about racial equality, how the North came to embrace the Republican party, and how Northerners viewed the secession crisis. Newspaper editorials comprise one portion of these documents. Such editorials help historians track changing political opinions throughout the nation. One must remember, however, that most newspapers of the period were financed by the parties themseleves, so their comments on the popularity of the various parties and the merits of their positions on the issues must be scrutinized with caution. Included also is an excerpt from Charles Sumner's famous Senate address "The Crime Against Kansas." Congressional oration and campaign speeches (often reprinted as campaign pamphlets) were another means through which the parties and their candidates put their views before the electorate. Again, however, the careful historian must ask whether such speeches shaped public opinion, or instead reflected politicians' attempts merely to say what the voters wanted to hear.

Nativism and Slavery

These editorials from a Pennsylvania Know Nothing newspaper reflect the importance of both anti-slavery and anti-Catholicism to the Know Nothing party. In the first, the editor describes the anti-slavery credentials of his party, using the term "Sam" to refer to the Know Nothing party (Know Nothings said that their founder was "Young Sam," nephew of "Uncle Sam"). The Horace Greeley referred to is the editor of the New York Tribune, *who was a well-known foe of slavery. In the other editorial, the editor complains that immigrant (especially Catholic) voters were responsible for electing Democrat Franklin Pierce as president in 1852 and Democrat William Bigler as governor of Pennsylvania in 1851. The editor predicts that the recent successes of the Know Nothings will diminish immigrants' excessive political influence. These editorials demonstrate that the Know Nothings used both anti-slavery and anti-Catholicism to appeal to Northern voters. This combination of issues made the Know Nothings a potent and popular alternative to the Republicans, who from 1854 to 1856 focused exclusively on preventing the extension of slavery. By emphasizing these issues, the Know Nothings won over a majority of the Whig party's former adherents and doomed that party to extinction, precipitating the first stage of the political crisis of the 1850s. Excerpted from the* Harrisburg Telegraph and Journal, *December 20 and 27, 1854.*

What are "Sam's" Principles?

December 20, 1854

The *New York Tribune* regards Know Nothingism as "a pro-slavery movement," designed to crush out the anti-slavery sentiment of the north; and the *Washington Union*, the organ of the National Administration, denounces it as "a Whig trick," intended to play "smash" with things in general, and the Democratic party in particular. Both these papers evidently dislike "Sam," although they don't understand his principles, or comprehend his real designs. If Know Nothingism is "a pro-slavery movement" and "a Whig trick," how happens it that Gov. Baker, of New Hampshire, who is a Democrat and a Know Nothing, is an active member and chairman of a board of directors of a Kansas Emigration Society, in Concord, the design of which is to save the new territory from Slavery? When a *Democratic* standard bearer in the "old Granite State" is a Know Nothing, and thus openly acts with the opponents of Slavery; and when an anti-Nebraska man like Morrison, is unanimously re-nominated for Congress, at a Convention presided over by Moses Norris, one of the "pillars of Democracy," it is very evident that Know Nothingism is neither "a pro-slavery movement," nor "a Whig trick." In Massachusetts, where the Know Nothings elected the Governor, and all the Senators, Representatives and Congressmen, there is not a solitary Nebraska man among them. Does this look like a "pro-slavery movement?" So in Pennsylvania, Ohio, Indiana, New York and other northern and western States, where the Know Nothings influenced the elections, Nebraskaism and slavery extension have been repudiated and crushed out. In every instance where Know Nothingism has triumphed, the result has been an emphatic verdict against the Nebraska swindle. At the South, as well as at the North, we find Know Nothingism arrayed against the Nebraska bill. "Sam" is eminently *national* in his principles, and repudiating all the *sectional isms* of the day, he deprecates any further useless and unprofitable agitation of the slavery question. He is willing that slavery shall remain where it is, and that the "peculiar institution" of our Southern friends shall not be interfered with; but at the same time he sets his face like flint against the *extension* of slavery to territory now belonging to or hereafter to come into this Union. "Sam" is just as sound on the anti-slavery question as Horace Greeley (but not quite so much of a *fanatic*), and has accomplished more in one year towards the overthrow of the "northern party with southern principles," than Greeley, with his ultraism and fanaticism, could do were he to live to the age of Methuselah.

More Facts for Americans

December 27, 1854

The dangers that menace our country from "the insidious wiles of *foreign* influence," are becoming so palpably evident, as to be perceptible to the most causal observer. It is an alarming fact–demonstrated by the most reliable statistics–that at this very time *foreigners* have the power to influence not only our State and local elections, but to *decide the election of President of the United States.*–

Let Americans look at the *facts*, as presented in the following statistics of fourteen States, taken from the last census by the *National Organ* at Washington city:

States	Foreign population	Foreign vote	Pierce's majority	Elect'l vote for Pierce
New York	655,224	93,317	27,201	35
Pennsylvania	303,105	43,300	19,446	27
Maryland	51,011	7,287	4,945	8
Louisiana	67,308	9,615	1,892	6
Missouri	76,570	10,938	7,698	9
Illinois	111,860	15,980	15,653	11
Ohio	218,099	31,157	16,694	23
Wisconsin	110,471	15,781	11,418	5
Iowa	20,968	2,995	1,180	4
Rhode Island	23,832	3,404	1,109	4
Connecticut	38,374	5,482	2,890	6
Delaware	5,243	749	25	8
New Jersey	59,804	8,543	5,749	7
California	<u>21,628</u>	<u>10,000</u>	<u>5,694</u>	<u>4</u>
		258,548	120,094	152

A careful examination of the foregoing statement will show that the foreign vote was larger than the majority given for Pierce, and that the aggregate foreign vote of these States is more than the whole number of the aggregate of Pierce's majorities in said States. If therefore, the foreign vote had been about equally divided, Gen. Scott would have been elected President of the United States. The *foreign Roman Catholics*, under the lead of their Bishops and Priests, voted to a man for Pierce, and elected him. The same class of voters went *en masse* for Gov. Bigler, and elected him Governor of this State. In this way, by concentrating their strength, they have controlled our elections for years, and would continue to do so, had not the American people discovered the danger that menaced them from this foreign Popish influence, and banded together for the protection of their liberties and institutions.

The Crime Against Sumner and the Emergence of the Republican Party

In May 1856, Massachusetts Senator Charles Sumner delivered a speech before the Senate popularly know as "The Crime Against Kansas," whose harsh criticism of South Carolina Senator Andrew P. Butler precipitated the assault upon Sumner a few days later by Butler's nephew, representative Preston Brooks. These excerpts focus upon Sumner's comments about Butler, but also reflect the passion driving the most radically anti-slavery wing of the Republican party. Brooks' subsequent attack upon Sumner left the Massachusetts Senator unconscious in a pool of blood. He did not return to the Senate for three years, becoming a "living martyr" to the anti-slavery cause. The attack upon Sumner seemed to prove the Republican charge that the South would stop at nothing to spread slavery and would not even allow civilized debate on the issue. The violence directed at Sumner convinced many Northerners to abandon the Know Nothing party for the Republican cause, as it seemed to indicate that the "Slave Power" posed a more immediate menace than immigrants and Catholics. This helped the Republicans replace the Know Nothings as the most powerful party in the North, initiating the second phase of the political crisis. Excerpted from the New York Tribune, *May 21 and 22, 1856.*

The Crime Against Sumner

May 21, 1856

My task will be divided under three different heads; *first*, THE CRIME AGAINST KANSAS, is its origin and extent; *secondly*, THE APOLOGIES FOR THE CRIME; and *thirdly*, the TRUE REMEDY.

But, before entering upon the argument, I must say something of a general character, particularly in response to what has fallen from Senators who have raised themselves to eminence on this floor in championship of human wrongs; I mean the Senator from South Carolina, [Mr. Butler,] and the Senator from Illinois, [Mr. Douglas,] who, though unlike as Don Quixote and Sacho Panza, yet, like this couple, sally forth together in the same adventure. I regret much to miss the elder Senator from his seat; but the cause, against which he has run a tilt, with such activity of animosity, demands that the opportunity for exposing him should not be lost; and it is for the cause that I speak. The Senator from South Carolina has read many books of chivalry, and believes himself a chivalrous knight, with sentiments of honor and courage. Of course he has chosen a mistress to whom he has made his vows, and who, though ugly to others, is always lovely to him; though polluted in the sight of the world, is chaste in his sight–I mean the harlot, Slavery. For her, his tongue is always profuse in words. Let her be impeached in character, or any proposition made to shut her out from the extension of her wantonness, and no extravagance of manner or hardihood of assertion is then too great for this Senator. The frenzy of *Don Quixote*, in behalf of his wench Dulcinea del Toboso, is all surpassed. The asserted rights of Slavery, which shock equality of all kinds, are cloaked by a fantastic claim of equality. If the slave States cannot enjoy what, in mockery of the great fathers of the Republic, he misnames equality under the Constitution–in other words, the full power in the National Territories to compel fellow-men to unpaid toil, to separate husband and wife, and to sell little children at the auction block–then, sir, the chivalric Senator will conduct the State of South Carolina out of the Union! Heroic knight! Exalted Senator! A second Moses come for a second exodus!

May 22, 1856

With regret, I come again upon the Senator from South Carolina (Mr. Butler), who, omnipresent in this debate, overflowed with rage at the simple suggestion that Kansas had applied for admission as a State; and, with incoherent phrases, discharged the loose expectoration of his speech, row upon her Representative and then upon her people. There was no extravagance of the ancient Parliamentary debate which he did not repeat; nor was there any possible deviation from truth which he did not make, with so much of passion, I am glad to add, as to save him from the suspicion of intentional aberration. But the Senator touches nothing which he does not disfigure–with error, sometimes of principle, sometimes of fact. He shows an incapacity of accuracy, whether in stating the Constitution or in stating the law, whether in the details of statistics or the diversions of scholarship. He cannot open his mouth but out there flies a blunder. Surely he ought to be familiar with the life of Franklin; and yet he referred to this household character, while acting as agent of our fathers in

England, as above suspicion; and this was done that he might give point to a false contrast with the agent of Kansas—not knowing that, however, they may differ in genius and fame, in this experience they are alike; that Franklin, when intrusted with the petition of Massachusetts Bay, was assaulted by a foul-mouthed speaker, where he could not be heard in defense, and denounced as a "thief," even as the agent of Kansas has been assaulted on this floor, and denounced as a "forger." And let not the vanity of the Senator be inspired by the parallel with the British statesmen of that day; for it is only in hostility to Freedom that any parallel can be recognized. But it is against the people of Kansas that the sensibilities of the Senator are particularly aroused. Coming, as he announces, "from a State"—aye, Sir, from South Carolina—he turns with lordly disgust from this newly-formed community, which he will not recognize even as "a body politic." Pray, Sir, by what title does he indulge in this egotism? Has he read the history of "the State" which he represents? He cannot surely have forgotten its shameful imbecility from Slavery, confessed throughout the Revolution, followed by its more shameful assumptions for Slavery since. He cannot have forgotten its wretched persistence in the slave trade as the very apple of the eye, and the condition of its participation in the Union. He cannot have forgotten its Constitution, which is republican only in name, confirming power in the hands of the few, and founding the qualifications of voters on "a settled freehold estate and ten negroes."

In all this sympathy there is strength. But in the cause itself there is angelic power. Unseen of men, the great spirits of History combat by the side of the people of Kansas, breathing a divine courage. Above all towers the majestic form of Washington once more, as on the bloody field, bidding them to remember those rights of Human Nature for which the War of Independence was waged. Such a cause, thus sustained, is invincible. It may be crushed to earth for day, but it will surely rise to grasp the victory. The contest which, beginning in Kansas, has reached us, will soon be transferred from Congress to a broader stage, where every citizen will be not only spectator, but actor; and to their judgment I confidently appeal. To the People, now on the eve of exercising the electoral franchise in choosing a Chief Magistrate of the Republic, I appeal, to vindicate the electoral franchise in Kansas. Let the ballot-box of the Union, with multitudinous might, protect the ballot-box in that Territory. Let the voters everywhere, while rejoicing in their own rights, help to guard the equal rights of distant fellow citizens; that the shrines of popular institutions, now desecrated, may be sanctified anew; that the ballot-box, now plundered, may be restored; and that the cry," I am an American citizen," may not be sent forth in vain against outrage of every kind. In just regard for Free labor in rage of every kind. In just regard for Free labor in that Territory, which it is sought to blast by unwelcome association with slave labor; in Christian sympathy with the slave, whom it is proposed to task and sell there; in stern condemnation of the Crime which has been consummated on that beautiful soil; in rescue of fellow-citizens, now subjected to tyrannical Usurpation; in dutiful respect for the early Fathers, who aspirations are now ignobly thwarted; in the name of the Constitution, which has been outraged—of the Laws trampled down—of Justice banished—of Humanity degraded—of Peace destroyed—of Freedom crushed to earth; and in the name of the Heavenly Father, whose service is perfect Freedom, I make this last appeal.

The Lincoln-Douglas Debates

In the nineteenth century, state legislatures chose U.S. senators. Hoping to improve their chances of unseating incumbent Stephen A. Douglas, Illinois Republicans in 1858 took the unusual step of announcing in advance that their Senate candidate in 1859 would be Springfield attorney Abraham Lincoln. They hoped that such an announcement would help Republicans win enough legislative races to unseat Douglas, whose popularity had recently increased when he refused to support Democratic moves to admit Kansas as a slave state. Lincoln challenged Douglas to a series of debates in a bold attempt to sway voters to the Republican cause, and Douglas accepted. In each debate, the first orator spoke for ninety minutes on any subject, his opponent would have two hours to respond, and then the first speaker would speak for thirty more minutes—a far cry from the "sound bites" of modern political discourse! One of the recurring themes of the debates was the place of blacks in American society, as Douglas repeatedly charged that Lincoln and the Republicans believed in the equality of the races. Lincoln's responses to

Douglas's allegation reflect a surprising racism. In part because of Lincoln's skillful debating, Republicans captured a majority of the Illinois votes cast in 1858. But because many of the legislators who would choose the Senator were Democrats not up for re-election in that year, Douglas retained his Senate seat. Nonetheless, the Republicans' strong showing in 1858 in Illinois (as well as other conservative "Lower North" states such as Indiana and Pennsylvania) indicated that Republican attempts to appear more moderate—the third key element of the political crisis of the 1850s—had succeeded. Lincoln's strong showing also helped him capture the Republican nomination for president in 1860 from New York's more radical William H. Seward. Excerpted from Robert W. Johannsen, ed., The Lincoln-Douglas Debates of 1858 *(New York, 1965), 52-53, 64-65, 127-9, 162-3.*

In the first debate, Lincoln replied to Douglas's charge that the Republicans sought racial equality as follows, and then went on the offensive with a critique of Douglas's position on the Dred Scott *decision:*

I will say here, while upon this subject, that I have no purpose, directly or indirectly, to interfere with the institution of slavery in the States where it exists. I believe I have no lawful right to do so, and I have no inclination to do so. I have no purpose to introduce political and social equality between the white and the black races. There is a physical difference between the two, which, in my judgment, will probably forever forbid their living together upon the footing of perfect equality, and inasmuch as it becomes a necessity that there must be a difference, I, as well as Judge Douglas, am in favor of the race to which I belong having the superior position. I have never said anything to the contrary, but I hold that, notwithstanding all this, there is no reason in the world why the negro is not entitled to all the natural rights enumerated in the Declaration of Independence, the right to life, liberty, and the pursuit of happiness. I hold that he is as much entitled to these as the white man. I agree with Judge Douglas he is not my equal in many respects–certainly not in color, perhaps not in moral or intellectual endowment. But in the right to eat the bread, without the leave of anybody else, which his own hand earns, *he is my equal and the equal of Judge Douglas, and the equal of every living man. . . .*

. . . I ask the attention of the people here assembled and elsewhere, to the course that Judge Douglas is pursuing every day as bearing upon this question of making slavery national. Not going back to the records, but taking the speeches he makes, the speeches he made yesterday and day before, and makes constantly all over the country—I ask your attention to them. In the first place, what is necessary to make the institution national? Not war. There is no danger that the people of Kentucky will shoulder their muskets, and, with a young nigger stuck on every bayonet, march into Illinois and force them upon us. There is no danger of our going over there and making war upon them. Then what is necessary for the nationalization of slavery? It is simply the next Dred Scott decision. It is merely for the Supreme Court to decide that no *State* under the Constitution can exclude it, just as they have already decided that under the Constitution neither Congress nor the Territorial Legislature can do it. When that is decided and acquiesced in, the whole thing is done. . . .

. . . This man sticks to a decision which forbids the people of a Territory from excluding slavery, and he does so not because he says it is right in itself—he does not give any opinion on that—but because it has been *decided by the court*, and being decided by court, he is, and you are bound to take it in your political action as *law*—not that he judges at all of its merits, but because a decision of the court is to him a *"Thus saith the Lord."* He places it on that ground alone, and you will bear in mind that, thus committing himself unreservedly to this decision *commits him to the next one* just as firmly as to this. He did not commit himself on account of the merit or demerit of the decision, but it is a *Thus saith the Lord*. The next decision, as much as this, will be a *Thus saith the Lord*. There is nothing that can divert or turn him away from this decision. It is nothing that I point out to him that his great prototype, Gen. Jackson, did not believe in the binding force of decisions. It is nothing to him that Jefferson did not so believe. I have said that I have often heard him approve of Jackson's course in disregarding the decision of the Supreme Court pronouncing a National Bank constitutional. He says, I

did not hear him say so. He denies the accuracy of my
recollection. I say he ought to know better than I, but I will
make no question about this thing, though it still seems to
me that I heard him say it twenty times. I will tell him
though, that he now claims to stand on the Cincinnati
platform, which affirms that Congress *cannot* charter a
National Bank, in the teeth of that old standing decision
that Congress *can* charter a bank. . . .

In response a few weeks later, Douglas set forth his own views on the
Dred Scott *decision and the place of blacks in American society:*

Mr. Lincoln objects to that decision, first and mainly
because it deprives the negro of the rights of citizenship. I
am as much opposed to his reason for that objection as I
am to the objection itself. I hold that a negro is not and
never ought to be a citizen of the United States. I hold that
this Government was made on the white basis, by white
men, for the benefit of white men and their posterity
forever, and should be administered by white men and
none others. I do not believe that the Almighty made the
negro capable of self-government. I am aware that all the
Abolition lecturers that you find traveling about through
the country, are in the habit of reading the Declaration of
Independence to prove that all men were created equal
and endowed by their Creator with certain inalienable
rights, among which are life, liberty, and the pursuit of
happiness. Mr. Lincoln is very much in the habit of following in the track of Lovejoy in this particular, by reading that part of the Declaration of Independence to prove
that the negro was endowed by the Almighty with the
inalienable right of equality with white men. Now, I say
to you, my fellow-citizens, that in my opinion, the signers
of the Declaration had no reference to the negro whatever,
when they declared all men to be created equal. They
desired to express by that phrase white men, men of
European birth and European descent, and had no reference either to the negro, the savage Indians, the Fejee, the
Malay, or any other inferior and degraded race, when
they spoke of the equality of men. One great evidence that
such was their understanding, is to be found in the fact
that at that time every one of the thirteen colonies was a

slaveholding colony, every signer of the Declaration represented a slaveholding constituency, and we know that no one of them emancipated his slaves, much less offered citizenship to them when they signed the Declaration; and yet, if they intended to declare that the negro was the equal of the white man, and entitled by divine right to an equality with him, they were bound, as honest men, that day and hour to have put their negroes on an equality with themselves. Instead of doing so, with uplifted eyes to heaven they implored the divine blessing upon them, during the seven years' bloody war they had to fight to maintain that Declaration, never dreaming that they were violating divine law by still holding the negroes in bondage and depriving them of equality.

My friends, I am in favor of preserving this Government as our fathers made it. It does not follow by any means that because a negro is not your equal or mine, that hence he must necessarily be a slave. On the contrary, it does follow that we ought to extend to the negro every right, every privilege, every immunity which he is capable of enjoying, consistent with the good of society. When you ask me what these rights are, what their nature and extent is, I tell you that that is a question which each State of this Union must decide for itself. Illinois has already decided the question. We have decided that the negro must not be a slave within our limits, but we have also decided that the negro shall not be a citizen within our limits; that he shall not vote, hold office, or exercise any political rights. I maintain that Illinois, as a sovereign State, has a right thus to fix her policy with reference to the relation between the white man and the negro; but while we had that right to decide the question for ourselves, we must recognize the same right in Kentucky and in every other State to make the same decision, or a different one. Having decided our own policy with reference to the black race, we must leave Kentucky and Missouri and every other State perfectly free to make just such a decision as they see proper on that question.

Lincoln found that voters in the closely contested central and southern portions of Illinois were being swayed by Douglas's charges that Lincoln

and the Republicans would bring about racial equality and integration.
Consequently, the Republican felt compelled to revisit this issue at the
beginning of the next debate:

Ladies and Gentlemen: It will be very difficult for an audience so large as this to hear distinctly what a speaker says, and consequently it is important that as profound silence be preserved as possible.

While I was at the hotel to-day, an elderly gentleman called upon me to know whether I was really in favor of producing a perfect equality between the negroes and white people. While I had not proposed to myself on this occasion to say much on that subject, yet as the question was asked me I thought I would occupy perhaps five minutes in saying something in regard to it. I will say then that I am not, nor ever have been, in favor of bringing about in any way the social and political equality of the white and black races—that I am not nor ever have been in favor of making voters or jurors of negroes, nor of qualifying them to hold office, nor to intermarry with white people; and I will say in addition to this that there is a physical difference between the white and black races which I believe will forever forbid the two races living together on terms of social and political equality. And inasmuch as they cannot so live, while they do remain together there must be the position of superior and inferior, and I as much as any other man am in favor of having the superior position assigned to the white race. I say upon this occasion I do not perceive that because the white man is to have the superior position the negro should be denied every thing. I do not understand that because I do not want a negro woman for a slave I must necessarily want her for a wife. My understanding is that I can just let her alone. I am now in my fiftieth year, and I certainly never have had a black woman for either a slave or a wife. So it seems to me quite possible for us to get along without making either slaves or wives of negroes. I will add to this that I have never seen, to my knowledge, a man, woman or child who was in favor of producing a perfect equality, social and political, between negroes and white men. . . . I will also add to the remarks I have made (for I am not going to enter at large upon this subject), that I have never had the least apprehension that I or my friends would marry negroes if there was no law to keep them from it; but as Judge Douglas and his friends seem to be in great apprehension that they might, if there were no law to keep them from it, I give him the most solemn pledge that I will to the very last stand by the law of this State, which forbids the marrying of white people with negroes. I will add one further word which is this: that I do not understand that there is any place where an alternation of the social and political relations of the negro and the white man can be made except in the State Legislature–not in the Congress of the United States–and as I do not really apprehend the approach of any such thing myself, and as Judge Douglas seems to be in constant horror that some such danger is rapidly approaching, I propose as the best means to prevent it that the Judge be kept at home and placed in the State Legislature to fight the measure. I do not propose dwelling longer at this time on this subject.

Northern Opinion on the Eve of Conflict

The following editorials, from the two most widely read and influential newspapers in the nation, remind us that the North was far from united in support of Lincoln and the Republican party in 1860. In the first, the New York Herald *warns that the "black republican" party (the* Herald *so disdained the Republicans that it refused even to capitalize their name) is foolishly dragging the nation into war by threatening the perpetuation of slavery, which the paper holds "is neither an evil nor a crime." The* New York Tribune, *in contrast, argues that Southern threats to secede are empty ones, another attempt by the "Slave Power" to bully the North into submission. The* Tribune *was especially popular in the Midwest, where its weekly national edition brought farmers news about Washington politics and plenty of Republican campaign propaganda. Such comments also emboldened the South, intensifying the polarization that marked the final stage of the political crisis. The* Herald's *stance convinced Southern politicians that many Northerners espoused their pro-*

slavery views and that the Republicans were fanatics who should be resisted. Editorials such as those in the Tribune pushed Southerners to make good on their long-standing promises to secede, rather than compromise and give the appearance that their threats had been empty ones.

Excepted from the New York Herald, October 19, 1860, and the New York Tribune, November 2, 1860.

The Northern Idea and Southern Safety–The Coming Collision Between the North and South

It is already becoming evident that the progress of the black republican party in the Northern and Central States is carrying this confederation to the very verge of a fearful abyss, from which only the most sagacious wisdom and the purest patriotism can save it.

Everywhere in the South the fires of resistance are already beginning to burn. Among the people a general feeling of apprehension is spreading, and the authorities and corporations of the several Southern States are already taking the initiative steps of action. It must not be supposed that the public men in the South, in announcing their adhesion to the idea of resistance to Northern aggression and dictation, are stirring the Southern people up to a point to which they advance unwillingly. Public men do not often lead public sentiment; they follow it, and reflect the tone and opinions of those around them, and in whose name they assume to speak. We must accept from the facts we already have in view the logical deduction that follows from them; in so doing we shall admit the conclusion that the general sentiment of the Southern people is strongly in support of the significant acts of their representative men. Hence the isolation and unconnected events which are occurring in different Southern localities must be read in a broad and comprehensive spirit, in order to grasp their true meaning and portent.

We published yesterday the proclamation of Gov. Gist of South Carolina, calling together the Legislature of that State for the purpose of electing Presidential electors, and providing, if advisable, for the safety of the State. The Legislature of Alabama provided, some time since, for the contingency of the election of a sectional President, by authorizing the Governor to call a State Convention immediately on the election of a black republican President becoming known. . . . [I]n many places in the South the young men are organizing themselves as minute men, to hold themselves at the orders of the Governors of their respective States.

These are alarming symptoms of the temper of the times, which no wise or prudent man will set aside with contempt, or even with inattention. It is a feeling which springs from the one great fact that no one can ignore. The black republican political organization is founded on one idea, from which its whole development proceeds; and this is, that "slavery is an evil and a crime." Politicians may disclaim any intent to do anything more but to exclude slavery from the Territories; public leaders may deny any wish to make war upon the institution in the States; and law abiding men may proclaim that they will act only within the terms and powers of the constitution; but these are professions which can be of no avail, for they are at war with the one all-pervading idea that underlies them. The natural and logical development of that idea makes the fulfillment of these impressions impossible. If slavery must be excluded from the Territories because it is an evil and a crime, the same results will apply to its exclusion from the States. If the moral sentiment of men must make war upon it in one place, it must do so in all places. Time and place make no excuse for palliating war against a moral evil or a social crime. If it is right at one time and in one place, it is right in all. This is the only logical result of the black republican creed, and to this it must come at last. . . .

The South hold, and hold rightly, that the institution of domestic servitude for the African race among them is neither an evil nor a crime. The greatest problem is, how shall four millions of an inferior race of men remain in society, best for their happiness, for the good of the community of which they form a part, and for the interests of civilization at large?

The Union is not about to be dissolved—the country is not going to the dogs—on the contrary, it is only a corrupt and played-out cabal of office-holders and Treasury leeches that are about to be turned off to get their living like honest folks or steal it a little less safely than they have done. That they should howl and perform all manner of unseemly antics, is but natural; but let them rest assured that the People laugh alike at their mock-fears for their country and their real concern for their precious selves. And so, "Good night to Marmion!"

How the Union Is to be Dissolved

Mr. George N. Sanders, one of Mr. Douglas's lieutenants, has sent us a manifesto showing how the Union is to be dissolved in case of Mr. Lincoln's election. Mr. Sanders professes to be opposed to Disunion, but is evidently not opposed to using the Fire-eaters' threats of it as a means of terrifying and bullying the Free States. We therefore print his bugaboo, and shall proceed to dissect it.

Mr. Sanders says:

> "All that the Union men of the South ask of you [Republicans] is to let the South alone."

Then, George, we are happy to assure you that there can be no chance for Disunion, for we are going to do that very thing. The South *will* be let alone by Mr. Lincoln's Administration–thoroughly, decisively, undeniably. Then what is there to secede on?

Mr. Sanders informs us that the Fire-eaters will not wait to see whether Mr. Lincoln purposes to do them any wrong or not. They will make their bolt under the rule of the Old Public Functionary, lest they should have no chance, or no excuse, after Mr. Lincoln's inauguration. And he adds that the Cotton States have already given us due and formal notice that they will secede in case of Mr. Lincoln's election.

We beg leave to assure Mr. S. that he is entirely mistaken as to the facts. The Cotton States have given no such notice, and they are not going to cut up any such didoes as he presages. A few noisy politicians have exhaled a large amount of unwholesome gas, but the Southern People regard their bravado with silent contempt. Jeff Davis & Co. tried to make Mississippi get ready for Secession nearly ten years ago; and the result was that Jeff was beaten for Governor of that State by so poor a tool as Henry S. Foote. Iverson & Co. tried the same game in Georgia, and were utterly routed under the lead of Howell Cobb. So Sam Houston badly thrashed the Fire-eating crew in Texas only last year. And if they put themselves in the way of another such exercise, they will get served worse in 1861 than they have ever yet been. There will be no call for Mr. Lincoln to put down rebellion and nullification in the South-West; the People of the Cotton States will do that whenever the opportunity is offered them. They are not going to have their mails stopped and their coast blockaded to gratify the mad ambition of a few self-seeking counterfeiters of Pro-Slavery fanaticism. We dare the Fire-eaters to submit the question of Secession or No Secession because of Lincoln's election to the popular vote of their own people. They will be badly beaten in every State but South Carolina, and probably beaten in he popular vote also. . . .

"But what will you do for Cotton?" ask the appalled Sanderses. Why, Sirs, we will buy it and pay for it, just as other nations do–just as we do now. They who grow or hold Cotton want to sell it just as much as those who spin and wear it want to buy it. Not to insist on the fact that the South already owes the North more than would keep the latter overstocked with Cotton for the next two years, we may observe that the South wants what we have to spare just as much as we want her Cotton. If she thinks she can enrich herself by levying an export duty of twenty-five per cent on her great staple, let her try it, by all means: the Cotton-growers of India, Africa, the West Indies and South America will be very much obliged to her. It will be a good thing also for those engaged in pushing the manufacture of flax and other vegetable fibers. Cotton would cease to be the staple of our Seceding States within five years, were they to levy an export duty of twenty-five per cent on it; and that might be better for the South and for mankind. We do not say it would, but it might be.

Rising U.S. Cotton Production

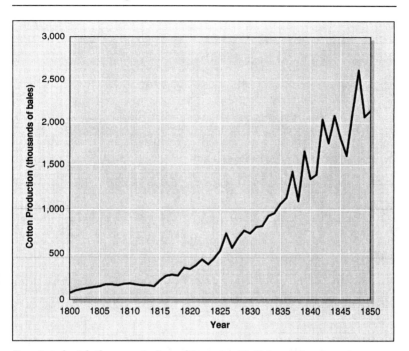

Reprinted with the permission of Prentice Hall from The American
Journey: A History of the United States, *Second Edition, by David
Goldfield, Carl Abbott, Virginia DeJohn Anderson, Jo Ann E.
Argersinger, Peter H. Argersinger, William L. Barney, and Robert M.
Weir. Copyright © 2001 by Prentice-Hall, Inc.*

Cotton Exports as Percentage of All U.S. Exports

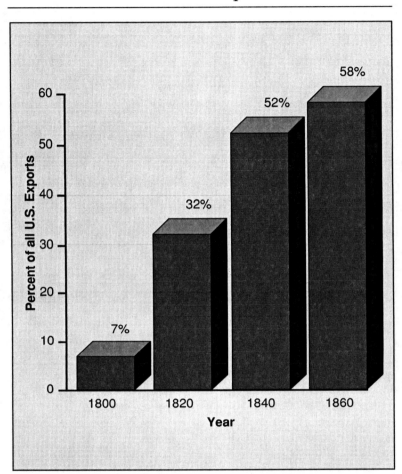

Number of Slaves Owned by Southerners

Source: U.S. Bureau of the Census.

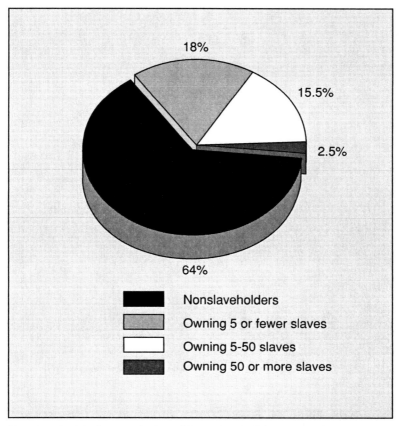

Reprinted with the permission of Prentice Hall from Out of Many: A History of the American People, *Third Edition, by John Mack Faragher, Mari Jo Buhle, Daniel Czitrom, and Susan H. Armitage. Copyright © 2000 by Prentice-Hall, Inc.*

Practice DBQ

Explain the causes and consequences of the American political crisis in the 1850s.

Remember that you should use your knowledge of American history and the primary sources in answering the Document-Based Question. You should take about forty-five minutes to complete your response.

Recommended Web Sites

---

http://www.dartmouth.edu/~dwebster/speeches/seventh-march.html
Copy of Daniel Webster's speech during the debate over the Compromise of 1850.

http://www.furman.edu/~benson/docs/seward.htm
William Henry Seward's "Higher Law" speech regarding the Compromise of 1850.

http://www.yale.edu/lawweb/avalon/fugitive.htm
Text of the Fugitive Slave Law of Compromise of 1850.

http://odyssey.lib.duke.edu/americavotes/buchanan.html
An image from James Buchanan's presidential campaign in 1856.

http://odur.let.rug.nl/~usa/D/1851-1875/dredscott/dredxx.htm
The U.S. Supreme Court decision in *Dred Scott v. Sanford*.

http://www.yale.edu/lawweb/avalon/dem1860.htm
Democratic Party platform in 1860.

http://www.theatlantic.com/politics/policamp/lowell.htm
Atlantic Monthly editorial in favor of Lincoln.

http://www.iath.virginia.edu/seminar/unit4/sumner.html
Charles Sumner's "Crime Against Kansas" address.

http://history.furman.edu/~benson/docs/sumenu.htm
Editorials about the caning of Charles Sumner.

http://history.furman.edu/~benson/docs/dsmenu.htm
Editorials about the Dred Scott case.

http://history.furman.edu/~benson/docs/jbmenu.htm
Editorials about John Brown's raid on Harper's Ferry.

Nat Turner and Slave Resistance

Merton L. Dillon

INTRODUCTION

Africans, who were forcefully brought to North America, did not willingly accept enslavement. They used every opportunity to prove to their "owners" that, even though the law considered them slaves, they still were human beings with wills of their own and that there were limits beyond which they would not allow themselves to be pushed. Most slaveowners accepted these limits as the price they had to pay for getting an acceptable amount of work from their labor force and for maintaining order on the plantation. Most slaves, in turn, learned that there also were limits to the degree of resistance that their owners—or the state—would tolerate. Outright defiance of authority or overt rebellion risked such severe punishment that only the bravest or most aggrieved dared undertake them. Thus life on every plantation was marked by tension between the slaves, who were trying to gain advantage in order to create a tolerable life for themselves, and the owners and overseers, who were trying to maintain strict control in order to run a profitable plantation. On rare occasions, this uneasy accommodation broke down, and violence, even revolt, was the result.

Slaves in the West Indies and in South America, like slaves in ancient Greece and Rome, carried out extensive uprisings. In contrast, only three such outbreaks occurred in North America: the Stono revolt in South Carolina (1739), the revolt in Louisiana (1811), and Nat Turner's revolt in Virginia (1831). Of these, Nat Turner's was the costliest in human life, for both races, and the most momentous in its impact on official policy and public opinion. It was also the most difficult for the white population to understand, first, because its leader apparently had been subjected to no unusually cruel treatment and, second, because the revolt was characterized by a messianic quality foreign to the experience of many, if not most, white people at the time.

150

SLAVE REVOLT AND
SLAVE VIOLENCE:
THEIR CAUSES AND CONSEQUENCE

Resistance to slavery, common throughout its existence, took various forms, each of them annoying and costly to the owners. Feigning illness, breaking or losing tools, slow or shoddy work, insolence, running away—these were only a few of the many unspectacular ways slaves exerted their independence and countered their owners' power.

Every slaveowner and every plantation experienced such resistance to some degree at one time or another. It apparently was inseparable from the institution itself. Rarer than any of these mundane forms of resistance, but more to be feared, was slave violence directed against whites. Most incidents of assault and murder resulted from identifiable grievances experienced by individual slaves; the motive appeared limited to personal revenge and retribution. In rare instances, however, slaves joined together in overt action calculated to damage, or even destroy, the institution of slavery itself and to free themselves from it. On those occasions when slaves organized revolts, they used violence to achieve a political rather than a personal end. North American slaves made only a few such attempts, and their success was nil, especially when compared with the more frequent, extensive, and long lasting revolts undertaken by slaves in the West Indies and in South America. The Stono Revolt in South Carolina (1739), the revolt in Louisiana (1811), and Nat Turner's revolt in Virginia (1831) practically exhaust the list. Each was limited in scope and readily put down. Nevertheless, each of them had important consequences for the slave community and for white southerners as well as for the future of slavery itself and of opposition to it. Of the three North American revolts, the one led by Nat Turner (sometimes called the Southampton revolt) is by far the best known and the most extensively documented. That revolt, like its predecessors, led to vicious reprisals against black people and to intensified efforts by slaveholders to make slavery more secure. In the North it contributed to the growth of an antislavery movement.

A Virginia State Official Explains Nat Turner's Revolt

John Floyd, governor of Virginia, pondering the causes of Turner's revolt, concluded that it resulted from influences other than those inherent in slavery itself. Here Floyd tells James Hamilton, Jr., the governor of South Carolina, his explanation of the revolt and the plan he will propose to prevent its repetition. Excerpted from The Southampton Slave Revolt of 1831, *ed. Henry Irving Tragle (Amherst, 1971), 275–76.*

Richmond
November 19, 1831

Sir:

I received your letter yesterday and with great pleasure will give you my impressions freely—

I will notice this affair in my annual message, but here only give a very careless history of it, as it appeared to the public—

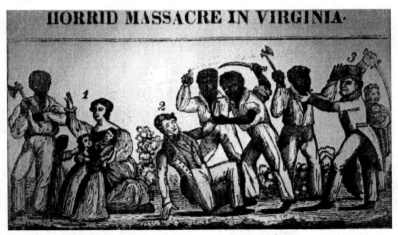

Nat Turner's revolt dramatized in a popular woodcut.

152

I am fully persuaded, the spirit of insubordination which has, and still manifests itself in Virginia, had its origin among, and eminated . . . from, the Yankee population, upon their *first* arrival amongst us, but mostly especially the Yankee pedlers and traders.

The course has been by no means a direct one—they began first, by making them religious—their conversations were of that character—telling the blacks God was no respecter of persons—the black man was as good as the white—that all men were born free and equal—that they cannot serve two masters—that the white people rebelled against England to obtain freedom, so have the blacks a right to do.

In the mean time, I am sure without any purpose of this kind, the preachers, principally Northern—were very assidious in operating upon our population, day and night, they were at work—and religion became, and is, the fashion of the time—finally our females and of the most respectable were persuaded that it was piety to teach negroes to read and write, to the end that they might read the Scriptures—many of them became tutoress in Sunday schools and, pious distributors of tracts, from the New York Tract Society.

At this point, more active operations commenced—our magistrates and laws became more inactive—large assemblages of negroes were suffered to take place for religious purposes—Then commenced the efforts of the black preachers, often from the pulpits these pamphlets and papers were read—followed by the incendiary publications of Walker, Garrison and Knapp of Boston, these too with songs and hymns of a similar character were circulated, read and commented upon—We resting in apathetic security until the Southampton affair.

From all that has come to my knowledge during and since this affair—I am fully convinced that every black preacher in the whole country east of the Blue Ridge was in [on] the secret, that the plans as published by those Northern presses were adopted and acted upon by them—that their congregations, as they were called knew nothing of this intended rebellion, except a few leading and intelligent men, who may have been head men in the Church—*the mass* were prepared by making them aspire to an equal station by such conversations as I have related as the first step.

Reprinted from *The Southampton Slave Revolt of 1831*, Henry I. Tragle, Editor. Amherst: The University of Massachusetts Press, 1971. Copyright © 1971 by Henry I. Tragle.

I am informed that they had settled the form of government to be that of white people, whom they intended to cut off to a man— with the difference that the preachers were to be their Governors, Generals and Judges. I feel fully justified to myself, in believing the Northern incendiaries, tracts, Sunday Schools, religion and reading and writing has accomplished this end.

I shall in my annual message recommend that laws be passed—To confine the Slaves to the estates of their masters— prohibit negroes from preaching—absolutely to drive from this State all free negroes—and to substitute the surplus revenue in our Treasury annually for slaves, to work for a time upon our Rail Roads etc etc and these sent out of the country, preparatory, or rather as the first step to emancipation—This last point will of course be tenderly and cautiously managed and will be urged or delayed as your State and Georgia may be disposed to co-operate.

In relation to the extent of this insurrection I think it greater than will ever appear. . . .

I am Sir,
with consideration and respect
your obt Sevnt
[obedient servant,]
s/John Floyd/

Religion as a Bulwark of Slavery

As Governor Floyd suggests, slaveowners generally did not object to their slaves being exposed to religious teachings. In fact, some viewed such instruction as one of their responsibilities, but, like Governor Floyd, they believed that in the "wrong" hands (as in Turner's), religion could be a subversive or revolutionary force. The following excerpt was written in 1842 by Lunsford Lane, a North Carolina slave. This memoir illustrates the use of religion for conservative ends. Excerpted from Five Slave Narratives: A Compendium *(New York, 1968), 20–21, with some minor grammatical corrections.*

I had never been permitted to learn to read; but I used to attend church, and there I received instruction which I trust was of some benefit to me. . . .

I often heard select portions of the scriptures read. And on the Sabbath there was one sermon preached expressly for the colored people which it was generally my privilege to hear. I became quite familiar with the texts, "Servants be obedient to your masters."— "Not with eye service as men pleasers."—"He that knoweth his master's will and doeth it not, shall be beaten with many stripes," and others of this class: for they formed the basis of most of these public instructions to us. The first commandment impressed upon our minds was to obey our masters, and the second was like unto it, namely, to do as much work when they or the overseers were not watching us as when they were. But connected with these instructions there was more or less that was truly excellent; though mixed up with much that would sound strangely in the ears of freedom. There was one very kind hearted Episcopal minister whom I often used to hear; he was very popular with the colored people. But after he had preached a sermon to us in which he argued from the Bible that it was the will of heaven from all eternity we should be slaves, and our masters be our owners, most of us left him; for like some of the faint hearted disciples in early times we said,—"This is a hard saying, who can bear it?"

Popular Reaction to Nat Turner's Revolt

Following revolts, retribution against African Americans, slave or free, guilty or innocent, was severe and indiscriminate and may help to account for the rarity of such revolts. The following newspaper report describes the aftermath of Nat Turner's revolt and the part that armed forces played in halting the reprisals. From the Constitutional Whig, *Richmond, Virginia, 3 September 1831, reprinted in* The Southampton Slave Revolt of 1831, *ed. Henry Irving Tragle (Boston, 1971), 69–70.*

It is with pain we speak of another feature of the Southampton Rebellion; for we have been most unwilling to have our sympathies for the sufferers diminished or affected by their misconduct. We allude to the slaughter of many blacks, without trial, and under circumstances of great barbarity. How many have thus been put into death (generally by decapitation or shooting) reports vary; probably however some five and twenty and from that to 40; possibly a yet larger number. To the great honor of General Eppes, he used every precaution in his power, and we

The presence of the troops from Norfolk and Richmond alone prevented retaliation from being carried much farther.

Popular Reaction to a Rumored Revolt in Louisiana

Solomon Northup, a slave in Louisiana during the 1840s, describes an abortive attempt by slaves to organize a mass escape to Mexico and the retaliation that followed. Note the apparent absence of a religious impulse for the revolt and the similarities with the aftermath of Nat Turner's revolt. Note, too, that the violence against slaves came to an end in a similar way. Abridged from Solomon Northup, Twelve Years a Slave: Narrative of Solomon Northup . . . *(Auburn, 1853), 246–49.*

The year before my arrival in the country there was a concerted movement among a number of slaves on Bayou Boeuf, that terminated tragically indeed. It was, I presume, a matter of newspaper notoriety at the time, but all the knowledge I have of it, has been derived from the relation of those living at that period in the immediate vicinity of the excitement. It has become a subject of general and unfailing interest in every slave-hut on the bayou, and will doubtless go down to succeeding generations as their chief tradition. Lew Cheney, with whom I became acquainted—a shrewd, cunning negro, more intelligent than the generality of his race, but unscrupulous and full of treachery—conceived the project of organizing a company sufficiently strong to fight their way against all opposition, to the neighboring territory of Mexico.

A remote spot, far within the depths of the swamp back of Hawkins' plantation, was selected as the rallying point. Lew flitted from one plantation to another, in the dead of night, preaching a crusade to Mexico, and, like Peter the Hermit, creating a furor of excitement wherever he appeared. At length a large number of runaways were assembled; stolen mules, and corn gathered from the fields, and bacon filched from smoke-houses, had been conveyed into the woods. The expedition was about ready to proceed, when their hiding place was discovered. Lew Cheney, becoming convinced of the ultimate failure of his project, in order to curry favor with his master, and avoid the consequences which he foresaw would follow, deliberately determined to sacrifice all his companions. Departing secretly from the encampment, he proclaimed among the planters the number collected in the swamp, and, instead of stating truly the object they had in view, asserted their intention was to emerge from their seclusion the first favorable opportunity, and murder every white person along the bayou.

Such an announcement, exaggerated as it passed from mouth to mouth, filled the whole country with terror. The fugitives were surrounded and taken prisoners, carried in chains to Alexandria, and hung by the populace. Not only those, but many who were suspected, though entirely innocent, were taken from the field and from the cabin, and without the shadow of process or form of trial, hurried to the scaffold. The planters on Bayou Boeuf finally rebelled against such reckless destruction of property, but it was not until a regiment of soldiers had arrived from some fort on the Texan frontier, demolished the gallows, and opened the doors of the Alexandria prison, that the indiscriminate slaughter was stayed. Lew Cheney escaped, and was even rewarded for his treachery. He is still living, but his name is despised and execrated by all his race throughout the parishes of Rapides and Avoyelles.

Such an idea as insurrection, however, is not new among the enslaved population of Bayou Boeuf. More than once I have joined in serious consultation, when the subject has been discussed, and there have been times when a word from me would have placed hundreds of my fellow-bondsmen in an attitude of defiance. Without arms or ammunition, or even with them, I saw such a step would result in certain defeat, disaster and death, and always raised my voice against it.

During the Mexican war I well remember the extravagant hopes that were excited. The news of victory filled the great house with rejoicing, but produced only sorrow and disappointment in the cabin. In my opinion—and I have had opportunity to know something of the feeling of which I speak—there are not fifty slaves on the shores of Bayou Boeuf, but would hail with unmeasured delight the approach of an invading army.

A Northern Editor Reacts to
Nat Turner's Revolt

Slave unrest obviously was primarily a southern problem, but Nat Turner's revolt led even northerners who were not abolitionists to worry about its probable effects on the nation at large. Here, a northern newspaper editor speculates on possible solutions to the "problem" of slave revolts. From the Ohio State Journal and Columbus Gazette, *October 20, 1831, 3.*

Since the suppression of the late Negro insurrection in Southampton county, Va. it appears that similar outrages have been attempted by the slaves and free colored people in different parts of North and South Carolina, Louisiana, Delaware, and the Eastern Shore of Maryland; and although the designs of the poor wretches concerned therein have been for the most part discovered and frustrated before much actual mischief had been done, yet the frequency of their late attempts has occasioned no little alarm in those parts of the union which have most to fear from a servile war. Whether these almost simultaneous movements in sections of the country so remote from each other be the result of accident, or of something like a preconcerted plan for a general insurrection among the slaves about this time does not fully appear. The latter supposition, however, is not altogether improbable; and although every man possessed of common sense will at once see that an attempt of this kind, however well matured, must ultimately result in the total extermination of at least all those engaged in it, if not of the entire colored population, yet, it is evident that it would inevitably occasion the loss of many valuable lives, and be productive of a vast amount of misery, before it could be suppressed.

A southern paper, speaking of these movements, and of the probability of their frequent recurrence so long as slavery shall be tolerated among us, suggests, whether it would not be right and expedient, after the National Debt shall have been paid, to apply the surplus revenue to the general emancipation of the slaves, and their removal beyond our territorial limits; and without intending to express an opinion, either as to the expediency or the feasibility of such a measure, we must say that it appears to us to be worthy of serious consideration. We believe that the people of these United States ought no longer to shut their eyes to the dreadful evils of slavery, and the consequences which, sooner or later, must inevitably result from it; and that the time has fully arrived when some plan should be devised for the removal of this curse from among us. We shall probably recur to the subject in a future number.

An Abolitionist Reacts to Nat Turner's Revolt

For many years before 1831, opponents of slavery had warned that slaves in the South would someday follow the example of the slaves in Saint-Domingue who successfully rebelled in the 1790s. In this selection, William Lloyd Garrison, the best known of the abolitionists, interprets Nat Turner's revolt as a fulfillment of that prophecy, calling for immediate emancipation as the only means to prevent a catastrophic race war for liberation. Abridged from William Lloyd Garrison, "The Insurrection," Liberator, Boston, September 3, 1831, 143.

What we have so long predicted,—at the peril of being stigmatized as an alarmist and declaimer,—has commenced its fulfilment. The first step of the earthquake, which is ultimately to shake down the fabric of oppression, leaving not one stone upon another, has been made. The first drops of blood, which are but the prelude to a deluge from the gathering clouds, have fallen. The first flash of the lightning, which is to smite and consume, has been felt. The first wailings of a bereavement, which is to clothe the earth in sackcloth, have broken upon our ears. . . .

True, the rebellion is quelled. Those of the slaves who were not killed in combat, have been secured, and the prison is crowded with victims destined for the gallows!

'Yet laugh not in your carnival of crime
Too proudly, ye oppressors!'

You have seen, it is to be feared, but the beginning of sorrows. All the blood which has been shed will be required at your hands. At your hands alone? No—but at the hands of the people of New-England and of all the free states. The crime of oppression is national. The south is only the agent in this guilty traffic. But, remember! the same causes are at work which must inevitably produce the same effects; and when the contest shall have again begun, it must be again a war of extermination. In the present instance, no quarters have been asked or given.

[Garrison now attempts to voice the slaveholders' justification for revenge against Nat Turner's band:]

But we have killed and routed them [the slaves] now. . . . We have the power to kill *all*—let us, therefore, continue to apply the whip and forge new fetters! . . . They were black—brutes, pretending to be men—legions of curses upon their memories! They were black—God made them to serve us! . . .

[Garrison, as an abolitionist, now addresses the slaveholders:]

Ye accuse the pacific friends of emancipation of instigating the slaves to revolt. Take back the charge as a foul slander. The slaves need no incentives at our hands. They will find them in their stripes—in their emaciated bodies—in their ceaseless toil—in their ignorant minds—in every field, in every valley, on every hill-top and mountain, wherever you and your fathers have fought for liberty—in your speeches, your conversations, your celebrations, your pamphlets, your newspapers—voices in the air, sounds from across the ocean, invitations to resistance above, below, around them! What more do they need? Surrounded by such influences, and smarting under their newly made wounds, is it wonderful that they should rise to contend—as other 'heroes' have contended—for their lost rights? It is *not* wonderful.

In all that we have written, is there aught to justify the excesses of the slaves? No. Nevertheless, they deserve no more censure than the Greeks in destroying the Turks, or the Poles in exterminating the Russians, or our fathers in slaughtering the British. Dreadful, indeed, is the standard erected by worldly patriotism!

For ourselves, we are horror-struck at the late tidings. We have exerted our utmost efforts to avert the calamity. We have warned our countrymen of the danger of persisting in their unrighteous conduct. We have preached to the slaves the pacific precepts of Jesus Christ. We have appealed to christians, philanthropists and patriots, for their assistance to accomplish the great work of national redemption through the agency of moral power—of public opinion—of individual duty. How have we been received? We have been threatened, proscribed, vilified and imprisoned—a laughing-stock and a reproach. Do we falter, in view of these things? Let time answer. If we have been hitherto urgent, and bold, and denunciatory in our efforts,—hereafter we shall grow vehement and active with the increase of danger. We shall cry, in trumpet tones, night and day,—Wo to this guilty land, unless she speedily repent of her evil doings! The blood of millions of her sons cries aloud for redress! IMMEDIATE EMANCIPATION can alone save her from the vengeance of Heaven, and cancel the debt of ages!

Slave Violence Directed against Individual Owners

Instances of slaves murdering their masters were frequent enough to cause concern even though slaveowners usually insisted that their own slaves could be trusted. Here, Mary Chesnut of South Carolina recounts the fate of two white women, one her acquaintance, the other her relative, who met their deaths at the hands of aggrieved slaves. Note that in each instance, the cause of the murders, as Mrs. Chesnut understands it, was not too much, but too little, discipline. How might the slaves' explanation for the murders differ from that given by Mrs. Chesnut? Excerpted from Mary Chesnut's Civil War, *ed. C. Vann Woodward (New Haven, 1981), 209–12.*

And now comes back on us that bloody story that haunts me night and day, Mrs. Witherspoon's murder.

The man William, who was the master spirit of the gang, once ran away and was brought back from somewhere west. And then his master and himself had a reconciliation, and the master henceforth made a pet of him.

The night preceding the murder, John Witherspoon went over to his mother's to tell her of some of William and Rhody's misdeeds. While their mistress was away from home, they had given a ball fifteen miles away from Society Hill. To that place they had taken their mistress's china, silver, house linen, &c&c. After his conversation with his mother, as he rode out of the gate, he shook his whip at William and said, "Tomorrow I mean to come here and give every one of you a thrashing."

That night Mrs. Witherspoon was talking it all over with her grandson, a half-grown boy who lived with her—slept, indeed, in a room opening into hers.

"I do not intend John to punish these negroes. It is too late to begin discipline now. It is all nonsense. I have indulged them past bearing, they all say. I ought to have tried to control them. It is all my fault. That's the end of it."

Mrs. Edwards, who was a sister of Mrs. Witherspoon, was found dead in her bed. It is thought this suggested their plan of action to the negroes. What more likely than she should die as her sister had done.

They were all in great trouble when John went off. William said, "Listen to me, and there will be no punishment here tomorrow." They made their plan, and then all of them *went to sleep,* William remaining awake to stir up the others at the proper hour.

What first attracted the attention of the family was the appearance of black and blue spots about the face and neck of the body of their mother. Then someone in moving the candle from the table at her bedside found blood upon their fingers. . . .

. . . [T]hey began to scent mischief and foul play in earnest, and they sent for the detective. Before he came they searched all houses and found bloody rags.

The detective dropped in from the skies quite unexpectedly. He saw that one of the young understrappers of the gang looked frightened and uncomfortable. This one he fastened upon and got up quite an intimacy with him. Finally he told this boy that he knew all about it. William had confessed privately to him to save himself and hang the others. But as the detective had taken a fancy to this boy, if he would confess everything, he would take him as state's evidence instead of William. The young man was utterly confounded at first but fell in the trap laid for him and told every particular from beginning to end.

Then they were all put in jail, the youth who had confessed among them, as he did not wish them to know of his *treachery* to them.

This was his story. "After John went away that night, Rhody and William made a great fuss—were furious at Mars John threatening them after all these years—to talk to them that away."

William said: "Mars John more than apt to do what he say he will do. You-all follow what I say and he'll have something else to think of beside stealing and breaking glass and china and table-cloths. If ole Marster was alive now, what would he say? Talk of whipping us at this time of day, &c&c."

Rhody kept the key of the house to let herself in every morning. So they arranged to go in at twelve. And then William watched, and they slept the sleep of the righteous.

Before that, however, they had a "rale fine supper and a heap of laughing at the way dey's all look tomorrow."

They smothered her with a counterpane [quilt] from a bed in the entry. He had no trouble the first time because they found her asleep and "done it all 'fore she waked." But after Rhody took her keys and went into the trunk and got a clean nightgown—for they had spoiled the one she had on—and fixed everything, candle, medicine, and all—she came to! Then she begged them hard for life. She asked them what she had ever done that they should want to kill her? She promised them before God never to tell on them. Nobody should ever know. But Rhody stopped her mouth by the counterpane. William held her head and hands down. And the other two sat on her legs. Rhody had a thrifty mind and wished to save the sheets and nightgown. She did not destroy them—they were found behind her mantelpiece. There the money was also, all in a hole made among the bricks behind the wooden mantelpiece.

A grandson of Rhody's slept in her house. Him she locked up in his room. She did not want him to know anything of this fearful night.

That innocent old lady and her gray hairs moved them not a jot.

Fancy how we feel. I am sure I will never sleep again without this nightmare of horror haunting me.

Mrs. Chesnut [Mary Chesnut's mother-in-law], who is their good angel, is and has always been afraid of negroes. In her youth the St. Domingo stories were indelibly printed on her mind.

She shows her dread now by treating everyone as if they were a black Prince Albert or Queen Victoria.

We were beginning to forget Mrs. Cunningham, the only other woman we ever heard of murdered by her negroes.

Poor Cousin Betsey was goodness itself. After years of free-dom and indulgence and tender kindness, it was an awful mistake to threaten them like children. It was only threats. Everybody knew she would never do anything.

How about Mrs. Cunningham? He [Mr. Cunningham] was an old bachelor, and the negroes had it all their own way till he married. And then they hated her. They took her from her room, just over one in which her son-in-law and her daughter slept. They smothered her, dressed her, and carried her out—all without the slightest noise—and hung her by the neck to an apple tree, as if she had committed suicide. Waked nobody in the house by all this. If they want to kill us, they can do it when they please—they are noiseless as panthers.

They were discovered—first, because dressing her in the dark, her tippet [nightcap] was put on hind part before. And she was supposed to have walked out and hung herself in a pair of brand-new shoes whose soles evidently had never touched the ground.

We ought to be grateful that any one of us is alive. But nobody is afraid of their own negroes. These are horrid brutes—savages, monsters—but I find everyone like myself, ready to trust their own yard. I would go down on the plantation tomorrow and stay there, if there were no white person in twenty miles. My Molly and half a dozen others that *I know*—and all the rest I believe—would keep me as safe as I should be in the Tower of London.

Slave Population as Percentage of Southern States

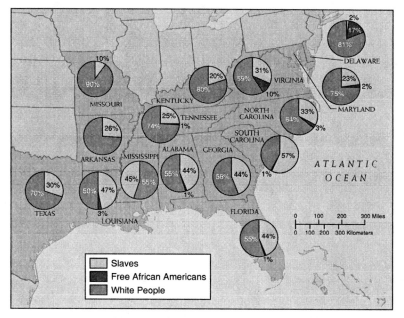

Reprinted with the permission of Prentice Hall from Out of Many: A History of the American People, *Third Edition, by John Mack Faragher, Mari Jo Buhle, Daniel Czitrom, and Susan H. Armitage. Copyright © 2000 by Prentice-Hall, Inc.*

Drawing: Nat Turner's Capture

Library of Congress

Practice DBQ

According to Americans in the nineteenth century, what factors led to violent slave rebellions?

Remember that you should use your knowledge of American history and the primary sources in answering the Document-Based Question. You should take about forty-five minutes to complete your response.

Recommended Web Sites

http://www.pbs.org/wgbh/aia/part4/index.html
Good historical documents on abolitionism and fugitive slaves.

http://vi.uh.edu/pages/mintz/primary.htm
A list of slave narratives on a variety of topics. See more slave narratives at http://docsouth.unc.edu/neh/texts.html and http://xroads.virginia.edu/~HYPER/wpa/wpahome.html.

http://digital.nypl.org/schomburg/images_aa19/
New York Public Library and Shomburg Center images of African Americans in the nineteenth century. Very good resource for images; the section on slavery (http://149.123.1.8/schomburg/images_aa19/slavery.cfm?rtya5845) is particularly helpful.

http://www.ups.edu/history/afamhis/longtxts/turner.htm
Full text of Nat Turner's confession.

http://amistad.mysticseaport.org/library/welcome.html
Primary documents relating to the *Amistad* case.

http://odur.let.rug.nl/~usa/D/1826-1850/slavery/fugitxx.htm
Testimony of escaped slaves in Canada.

http://www.furman.edu/~benson/docs/rcd-fmn1.htm
This document provides a defense of slavery based on the Bible.